WORSHIP, I

˙Dedication

To David Westlake. Your passion for God and its expression through worship, evangelism and justice has been an amazing inspiration. Your friendship, love, correction and loyalty over many years mean the world.

Worship, Evangelism, Justice

MIKE PILAVACHI
WITH LIZA HOEKSMA

survivor

ISBN 1 84291 284 4
13–ISBN 978–1–842912–84–3

Survivor is an imprint of
KINGSWAY COMMUNICATIONS LTD
Lottbridge Drove, Eastbourne BN23 6NT, England.
Email: books@kingsway.co.uk

Printed in the USA

Contents

Acknowledgements

We would like to thank many people who have helped us in understanding the issues that are expressed in this book.

The worship leaders with whom I have argued and discussed these issues: Matt Redman, Tim Hughes, Martyn Layzell, David Ruis, Jonny Parks and Onehundredhours. Also J. John, Bishop Graham Cray, Andrew Croft and David Pambakian for the hours of discussion on these subjects.

We would both like to thank those who have read the manuscript and given invaluable comments: Gemma Foster, Jonno Ives, Karen Layzell, Becca Sampson and Luke Williams. With particular thanks to Craig Borlase for his timely wisdom, editing skills and encouragement and to Daniel and Marlies Hoogteyling and Emily Vesey for sharing their experiences.

Special thanks to Martyn and Emily Layzell and Ali MacInnes for their friendship, love, encouragement and wisdom. It's a pleasure and a privilege to live life with you.

Lastly we would like to thank the church we are a part of and where all of this is worked out: Soul Survivor Watford – we love you very much.

INTRODUCTION: Love God, Love My Neighbour

This little book is written as a result of a journey my friends and I have been on these last few years. As we have studied the word of God and allowed Him to speak to us, we have realised that an artificial divide has been created between worship, evangelism and justice. This is a divide that has to end if we are to be a biblical people who obey God in all that we sing and say and do. They belong hand in hand, not like options that we pick and choose – 'today I'm focusing on evangelism, maybe next week it will be justice' – but working together, overlapping and impacting each other in a way I hadn't fully grasped.

I believe that worship is an event, an act. The Magi bowed down and worshipped the baby Jesus, and the 24 elders cast their crowns and worship before the Lion of the tribe of Judah. I believe that worship is also a way of life. To worship is to witness and to witness is to worship. God says that if we do not feed the hungry, He will not listen to our songs, yet if we look after people's physical needs without adoring God we are forgetting our first love. To care for the poor and to fight for justice without also bringing our thanksgiving and praise to God can and does lead to jaded exhaustion and bitterness.

I passionately believe these are important concepts for us to grasp and put into practice in our lives if we are to truly see the revival many have been praying so long for. This is the story of my journey into God's word and into God's world. I hope it will be yours also.

Living without dignity

South Africa is one of my favourite places. I love the breathtaking landscapes, the feeling of the sun on my face while standing on the sandy beaches that line the coast, the amazing wildlife, the taste of a good bunny chow (a curry that doesn't actually have anything to do with rabbits) and of course the wonderfully generous and loving people I have met there. It was also the place where God shared something of His heart with me in a way that I know has changed me for ever.

I often visit Durban, a city on the eastern coast which demonstrates one of the biggest contrasts of any culture you'll ever see. You have both the developed world and the developing world, extremes of rich and poor, living right on each other's doorsteps. Some people live in five-bedroom gated houses with their own swimming pools and tennis courts just a few miles from many children who have nothing and live on the street.

I'd often been told to be wary of the street kids, warned off with stories of how they steal, lie and cheat. People had told me that most of them are high on drugs, that they hang around the beaches causing a nuisance and are threatening the tourist industry. When I was there in February seven street boys stopped my friends and me and asked us for money. Not wanting to give them cash, we offered to buy them some food instead and as we waited in line for their burgers, chips and coke, we began to chat to them about how they ended up on the streets. We discovered that all of them were orphans with not a single living relative among them to take them in. Can you even imagine what that would be like? Not only to lose your parents but to have literally no one else to turn to? They had no choice; they had nowhere else to go but the streets. We found out the youngest was 13 and the eldest just 16. As they answered our questions we could see their own written all over their faces: 'Why are you asking all of this? What do you want from us?' They spent their days begging money from strangers but rarely did anyone want to actually talk to them, most just threw them some coins and left as quickly as they could. As we talked, the guys huddled close together, eyeing us suspiciously, their meals disappearing into their hungry stomachs in seconds. Something started stirring in my heart. 'We'll come and see you again tomorrow,' I said. They shrugged and turned away, unsure whether to believe us or not. The next day we went back and found them in the same place and hung out with them again, trying to find out more about them. We went back again and again over the week and gradually their reservations faded as they realised we intended them no harm and were only interested in getting to know them.

The first time we met Edwin, the youngest of the group, he was obviously high from glue-sniffing, but it took me until the end of the week to pluck up the courage to ask him why he did it. His response was very matter of fact: 'Because it takes away the pain.' There was nothing I could say to that. I had no right to tell him that what he was doing was damaging him, because

I've never known the depth of pain that drives someone to that level of self-destruction.

Eventually they trusted us enough to take us to their 'home'. It was on some wasteland that our South African friends had warned us not to go near because it was dangerous. I didn't know what to expect and felt almost nervous as we walked there. These young boys had made their home between two trees; it was just a cardboard box that they would climb into at night to go to sleep. It was a shocking reality to be confronted with compared to the comforts I took for granted. I felt sick to my stomach. But the one thing I'll never forget is what I saw on one of the branches above the box. There, swinging in the breeze, were about 20 coat hangers with absolutely nothing on them. The boys didn't have enough money to buy food, so of course there was no way they would have enough to buy a change of clothes. They'd worn the same filthy, ripped trousers and t-shirts every day we'd met them. They'd found the coat hangers discarded somewhere and they needed something that would make their cardboard box between two trees feel a little more like home, so they'd brought them back and hung them proudly. That disturbing image stayed with me during the four months before we were able to go back to South Africa again.

This time when they saw us the boys ran up to greet us smiling, their wariness completely gone. We wanted so much to help and had been trying to think of things we could do that would make a difference to their lives. My friend and I bought them each a pair of trainers and I cannot even begin to describe their joy; they didn't have one pair of shoes between them and now they were putting on brand new trainers. They jumped around, kicking their newly adorned feet high in the air, laughing and crying out with delight. They felt like kings, but we knew there were many more needs in their life that a pair of trainers wouldn't fix.

The next stop was the supermarket. I've never felt so rich or so privileged as walking in with these young guys and knowing that the things they so desperately needed were within my grasp to give. We'd intended to buy them food but also asked if there was anything else they wanted. They looked at each other and nodded; they were all agreed: the thing they wanted more than anything else was the strongest deodorant and soap that money could buy. I smiled at them as they scanned the shelves trying to work out which one would make them smell the best, but my heart was cracking. Yes, they needed food to give sustenance to their malnourished bodies, but they also needed dignity. They knew that they smelt bad, their bodies and clothes unwashed and uncared for, but they had no way of fixing that problem themselves. They just had to accept it as a part of their lives that when they were around other people, noses would be turned up, accompanied by a look of disgust they were powerless to change. With soap and deodorant that cost the equivalent of just a few pounds, they could feel human again – they could hold their heads that bit higher knowing they were able to take care of their bodies.

As we left the supermarket I noticed Edwin wasn't wearing his trainers. I asked why and the others said that he had hurt his leg and couldn't put them on. When I saw he was walking with a slight limp I asked if he'd been to a doctor and they laughed. What doctor would see them? Yet another thing I had taken for granted. So we took him to the local clinic, persuading the reluctant doctor to see him. I doubt you'll ever see anyone more excited to be seeing a doctor than Edwin. The ointment and bandage they used was like bestowing him with dignity and worth, and from that moment on I never saw him without the bandage. Even once his leg was healed he wore it like a medal, proud that he had been able to see a doctor and was worthy of medical treatment.

When the time came to say goodbye, as we were going back to the UK, they all hugged us and asked us to come and see them again. I promised we would be back in April and would come and find them, but it was agonising to leave them. Most nights when I climb into my comfortable bed and pull the duvet over me, I think of them and wonder whether they're still sleeping in the same box, between the same two trees, empty coat hangers above them, and I pray they're all still alive.

I'm not telling you what we did to make us sound good, because believe me, I know our offering was small. I believe God changed me through meeting these guys in a way that I wanted to share with you, as it has been a key step on my journey of faith. Meeting my friends who lived on the street in South Africa made me realise that God's heart for the poor also has to impact the life of anyone who wants to follow Him.

'Religion' is a dirty word

The church is no longer at the heart of the community. If someone is in trouble they may turn to friends and family, the government or even alcohol and drugs, but few would consider setting foot inside the church. While there have been encouraging signs of growth in pockets of the church, the overall number of people attending services has been declining for almost a century.

God has stayed the same so what has changed? Jesus'

message that has such a radical impact on people's lives still stands today. Meeting Him was enough to turn people's lives around and cause them to leave everything behind to follow Him, but now He is often dismissed as a charismatic political leader who died an untimely death.

Our society seems in many ways more open to spirituality, but we've decreased in our understanding of true faith. Religion has become a dirty word that even Christians don't want to be associated with; the mark of an institution that has been at the heart of war, conflict and condemnation rather than bringing a message of hope and peace.

This has been painful to watch for those of us who want to follow God with all our hearts, who know He is 'the way, the truth and the life' and want those around us to be living in the same freedom and love that we are. Society tells us that it has less and less room for God, and yet the pain and misery we see around us show there is perhaps a greater need than ever for all He brings. How do we reconcile these two extremes and help people to identify with God?

People who are fully devoted to God and desire to serve Him with all they have will surely impact this generation. As I've sought God and asked Him what I can do, how I can live my life for Him and how to better reflect Him to those around me, I've come back to the words of Jesus when asked what the greatest commandment was. He replied, 'Love the Lord your God with all your heart and with all your soul and with all your mind and with all your strength' (Mark 12:30). We can't get away from the fact that loving God and being in an intimate relationship with Him is our highest priority. It's the most precious thing we have and should be invested in and protected at all costs.

But when Jesus highlighted the greatest commandment He was quick to say, 'The second is this: "Love your neighbour as yourself"' (v. 31). With today's global society we may know more about the lives of people in Africa than we do about the people who actually live next door to us. We are in a time when we have easy access to all sorts of information and we can see TV pictures of disasters happening in India literally minutes after they have happened. We take this for granted, but it means our neighbour can be on the other side of the world and yet we are called to love them as ourselves.

Jesus told us that loving God and loving our neighbour should go hand in hand. We've often separated out our spiritual activities from our secular ones: we go to a home group, that's spiritual; we buy a pair of trainers, that's secular. Or is it? If we do our part to ensure that the person who is making our trainers gets a fair wage and works in reasonable conditions, isn't that an act of loving our neighbour and therefore a spiritual activity? God is interested in the whole of our lives and He wants access to everything so that we can make choices that reflect Him better.

We're going to explore the areas of worship, justice and evangelism as three key things on God's heart that we have often separated when they belong together. We'll be looking at what it means to worship God with all of your life and to love Him with your whole heart, what evangelism looks like in today's culture and what God's passion for justice means for us and how we can influence this world, which seems to be in such a terrible state.

I believe that worship, evangelism and justice are close to God's heart and that they belong together. If we continue to ignore them, or even separate them, we will continue to see the numbers of people following God decline and the church's voice grow weaker. If we bring them back together, could it be that the church will again be right at the heart of the community and God will again be worshipped as He deserves?

Part 1
WORSHIP

1

The Highest Priority

It may be easy to say that worship is our highest priority, but to really grasp why God is so keen on it we have to do a bit more digging around the subject. It's important for us to recognise what worship is really all about, why God instilled it as the most important thing for us to do, what happens when we let it slip and what happens when we offer God genuine worship. Our ultimate role model of the worship God requires is Jesus and we need to fully grasp just what His worship looked like in order to see how ours should follow. If we assume that God will be pleased if we just sing a few worship songs, we will be missing out on so much of God's blessing.

To understand the heart of worship we have to go right back to the beginning and look at the story of God creating human life. God is love and therefore He created us out of love and when He formed Adam and Eve He created them to live alongside Him in the Garden of Eden. It was only when they sinned that Adam and Eve became separated from Him as we are now. When they took the fruit of the knowledge of good and evil, the heart of their sin was that they wanted to be independent; God had specified just one tree as off-limits to them out of all that He had created and given to them. Their struggle was whether to obey God or to set their own rules; to believe that God knew what was best for them or to doubt His motives for keeping them from the tree; to walk away or to try and make themselves God-like in having knowledge of good and evil. We all know how the story goes: they took the fruit and in doing so they chose their own desires over obedience to God and placed a higher value on the things that God had created than on the Creator Himself.

That was the problem for Adam and Eve, for Israel throughout the Old Testament and in fact continues to be the fundamental issue for us even today. The problem has never been 'Will we worship?' We were created to worship, so it comes as naturally to us as breathing. The real question is, 'Who or what will we worship?' We think of idols as those weird objects carved out of wood from the Old Testament days and think that we would never be so stupid as to bow down to a piece of tree. The truth is that we worship things that are equally as powerless to help us, like money or TV. How? Because to make an idol out of something is simply to give it a higher priority in our lives than God. Worshipping God means putting Him first and remembering that He is more important than anything or anyone else.

Covenants

In early Old Testament times a battle would end with a covenant between the victor and the vanquished that set out how they would relate to one another. It wasn't quite the friendly chat over a cup of tea that it can sound like. The conqueror would set the terms of the agreement and the conquered would have to accept. The way to seal the deal was not with a handshake or messed up – they couldn't worship perfectly, so God in His great mercy established a new covenant. The basis of this new covenant was that He needed a perfect worshipper to offer perfect worship. Enter Jesus.

Jesus, as representative of the human race, took upon Himself the role of keeping the law perfectly. He worshipped and obeyed His Father and thus established the new covenant, the basis of which was that God kept both sides of the deal. He was both the conqueror and the conquered, He obeyed and was obeyed. Jesus fulfilled the requirement of perfect worship through living a life of perfect worship and dying a perfect death.

Jesus lived a life of true obedience before God – a claim that not a single one of us can make, no matter how holy a picture we try and paint to the people around us. While Jesus' death on the cross was many things – it was an atoning sacrifice to pay for our sins, it was the place where reconciliation occurred between God and humans, the place where we were freed from slavery to sin, it was the end of the power of death and the place where victory over Satan was won – the heart of what Jesus did on the cross was worship. The book of Hebrews describes Jesus' death on the cross as the one perfect sacrifice. If in the Old Testament a sacrifice was given as an act of worship, then the perfect sacrifice of Jesus was perfect worship. By Jesus' sacrifice of Himself He was doing more than saying, 'You, Creator God, are more important than Your creation,' because Jesus was so much more than just a token of creation. He was saying something even more complete: 'You the Creator are more important than life itself and so I will sacrifice life itself.'

The worship song on the cross

As part of that perfect worship and almost as if to underline the point, when on the cross Jesus used the words from a song of worship that was written hundreds of years earlier. It's called Psalm 22. The words that Jesus cried out on the cross are taken directly from the first line of Psalm 22: 'My God, my God, why have you forsaken me?' When we begin to see the psalm in this light, it is clear that although it is written by David it is undeniably about Jesus. Why don't you try reading the psalm while thinking about Jesus and the accounts of His crucifixion? I have pulled out some key verses here to show you what I mean.

'But I am a worm and not a man, scorned by men and despised by the people. All who see me mock me; they hurl insults, shaking their heads' (vv. 6–7). Compare this with verses from Matthew 27: 'They put a staff in his right hand and knelt in front of him and mocked him' (v. 29) and, 'Those who passed by hurled insults at him, shaking their heads' (v. 39).

'He trusts in the Lord; let the Lord rescue him. Let him deliver him, since he delights in him' (v. 8). This is a direct reflection of the fact that they mocked Jesus: 'Come down from the cross, if you are the Son of God!' (Matthew 27:40); 'He saved others . . . but he can't save himself!' (v. 41).

'From birth I was cast upon you; from my mother's womb you have been my God' (v. 10). If anyone had the right to say these words then it was not King David but the son of Mary.

'My strength is dried up like a potsherd, and my tongue sticks to the roof of my mouth; you lay me in the dust of death' (v. 15). It is obvious that your tongue sticks to the roof of your mouth when your mouth is dry and you are thirsty. On the cross Jesus cried out, 'I am thirsty' (John 19:28).

'...a band of evil men has encircled me, they have pierced my hands and my feet' (v.16). Of course we know that for Jesus to be placed on the cross they pierced His hands and feet with nails.

'They divide my garments among them and cast lots for my clothing' (v.18). Compare with: 'Dividing up his clothes, they cast lots to see what each would get' (Mark 15:24).

'I will declare your name to my brothers; in the congregation I will praise you' (v. 22). This verse is the most clear that the psalm is talking about Jesus. Why? Because in Hebrews 2:11–12 it says, 'So Jesus is not ashamed to call them brothers. He says, "I will declare your name to my brothers; in the presence of the congregation I will sing your praises."'

'For he has not despised or disdained the suffering of the afflicted one' (v. 24). Of the prophecies of Jesus we see in the Old Testament this one mirrors the words that describe the Suffering Servant in Isaiah 53, such as verse 3: 'He was despised and rejected by men, a man of sorrows, and familiar with suffering.' And the psalmist is telling us here that God did not despise the suffering of Jesus on the cross, but accepted it as pure worship.

And the best bit of this psalm? It's the ending. The song that began with the desperate cry of 'Why have you forsaken me?' ends with the words that bring hope and life to us all. Just five small words, but they're the difference between eternal life and death to us: 'For he has done it' (v. 31), echoed all those years later as Jesus died on the cross and declared, 'It is finished' (John 19:30).

The theological basis for worship

Jesus dying on the cross is the basis of the new covenant that brought us back into relationship with God. Although Jesus offered the perfect sacrifice of worship, that doesn't mean that we are no longer required to worship. Far from it.

As we know, Jesus told us that the greatest commandment is to 'Love the Lord your God with all your heart and with all your soul and with all your mind and with all your strength' (Mark 12:30) – a commandment given to Moses that still holds true for us today.

The Westminster Shorter Catechism (written way back in the seventeenth century) begins with the question: 'What is the chief end of man?' i.e. what is man's reason for being? The answer given? 'The chief end of man is to glorify God and enjoy Him forever.' This is simply a different way of expressing what Jesus had said was the most important commandment.

In Matthew 6 Jesus calls us to 'seek first [God's] kingdom' and I've heard it said that if you don't seek it first, you don't seek it at all. We can't have divided hearts. There's no room for saying, 'Lord, You are my God, but I just need to focus on my career right now,' or, 'I've got a new girlfriend, so once the relationship's a bit more established, I'll put You first again.' Jesus warns, 'No-one can serve two masters . . . you cannot serve both God and Money' (Matthew 6:24). And isn't this true for all areas of our lives? You can't serve God and your career. You can't serve God but put your family before Him. You can't serve God and place a higher value on security than Him. There's no room for more than one thing at the top of our priority list. If we put anything over and above God we see everything through the eyes of what our priority is. So, for example, if God asks us to be generous and our top priority is not pleasing God but keeping money and security for ourselves we will not obey God. God knows that for us to have maximum freedom and enjoyment of the life He's given us, we need to put Him first, to put everything we do through a filter of 'Does it please God's heart? Is it what He would have me do?' If the answer is not 'yes' on both counts then we shouldn't do it or we are following our own ways and setting our own rules. When God is at the top of the list, the other priorities seem to fall in line with His way of thinking, but if anything else creeps in above Him then we are breaking the first and most important command to love Him whole-heartedly.

'We never thought we could know God like this'

Worship has always been a core value of Soul Survivor, the charity I work for which seeks to encourage and equip young people in their walk with Jesus. We spend a long time in our meetings singing songs of love and praise to God, and while that's not a definition of worship, it is an expression of worship. There is a clear biblical principle for using music and songs in times of worship – in the Old Testament when psalms were sung at the temple, in the New Testament when we hear they sang 'psalms, hymns and spiritual songs' (Colossians 3:16) and in the glimpse we are shown of heaven with the songs sung by the elders, angels, living creatures and all of creation (Revelation 4–5).

But we have confused ourselves a little by saying things like, 'Now we'll have a time of worship', as someone at the front picks up a guitar and starts singing. Worship automatically becomes equated with music, but this is wrong, as the rest of the service – and indeed our lives – can be worship too. The singing is just a focus for the worship. There is a place for an act of worship and then a place for an outworking of that worship. We're going to be spending much of the rest of this book looking at that outworking, but first let's have a look at this act of worship through the singing of songs, and what happens when we do this.

At our church, Soul Survivor Watford, we put a large emphasis on singing songs of worship in our meetings, not because we're more musically talented than others, but because when we fell in love with Jesus that was the first way we wanted to express it. We wanted to tell Him how much He meant to us, to adore Him publicly and privately by singing words of love and praise, to give something back to Him for all that He had given to us. One thing we quickly discovered was that you can't out-give the Giver. As we sang to Him, He met with us in ways we'd never expected. As we told Him we loved Him, He was pouring more love into our hearts. As we proclaimed how worthy He was, He began to deal with our own sense of identity and instil in us the knowledge that we are His dearly loved sons and daughters. It seems that if you give to God, it pretty much goes against His nature not to give you something back and we found that as a congregation of worshippers we were being changed.

This idea that God does something in us as we offer Him our hearts was demonstrated to me so clearly a few years ago during a worship time at one of our summer events. I was standing by the side of the stage while Matt Redman was leading worship, when I felt someone come up and nudge me. As I turned round, a young guy pressed a knuckleduster into my hand. He gave a shy smile and walked off. He was swiftly followed by a teenager who offered me a knife, and not the kind of knife he would have needed for a few days' camping in Somerset. 'Could you get rid of this for me?' he asked. Bemused, I took it from him and carried on worshipping. Then another young guy approached me and handed me a number of small foil packets that I figured contained drugs. 'I don't need these any more,' he said. I put them in my pocket and wondered what else would be added to my collection by the end of the evening.

Later that night, after we'd finished the meeting, I showed Matt what I'd been given. Jokingly I took the small foil packets from my pocket and said, 'We could have a good smoke with these!' Matt looked down at my hand and when his eyes met mine again there was a look of amusement there: 'I'd like to see you try: they're condoms!' What a poor, sad, single Christian youth worker I was! But the point was not my ignorance (or innocence, as I prefer to view it), but that in the time leading up to those people coming up to me, no one had preached. No one had said, 'God doesn't want you to physically hurt people, so please give up your weapons,' or given an even more ambiguous call to 'give up the things that are holding you back from your relationship with God; the things you know He doesn't want you to be involved in any more'. And if we'd sung the line 'I will offer up my life and my condoms' then I had missed it. What we had done was worship together, and during that time the Holy Spirit was able to move in people's hearts. Jesus said of the Holy Spirit, 'He will convict the world of guilt in regard to sin and righteousness and judgement' (John 16:8).

Another group came one summer, bringing with them a stash of drugs. They had never met with Jesus before and had just fancied a few days away from their parents and thought

Soul Survivor would be a laugh. But then they came to the main meetings and got friendly with some of the Christians there. They came up to me at the end of the week and told me how they had given their lives to Jesus. With their new friends, they'd gone into a field, buried the drugs under the grass and asked their friends to pray for them as they became Christians. (I'm sure the cows in Somerset have never been quite the same since. . .)

Now, as a youth leader I've had to do 'The Sex Talk' more times than I care to remember, but what I've found is that no matter how much effort I put in, no matter how many times I make them promise not to mess up, the best way for them to understand where their boundaries should be is when they meet with Jesus. And it's the same when it comes to trying to persuade them not to use drugs, to smoke or to swear, or asking them to be nicer to each other: knowing Jesus and how He lived and how He wants them to live is the best encouragement they can get. Because it's not about the words we use; it's about knowing and loving Jesus. When we do, we can't help but want to be like Him and do what pleases Him. As Jesus said, 'If anyone loves me, he will obey my teaching. . . He who does not love me will not obey my teaching' (John 14:23–24).

As God meets with us and changes our hearts, we begin to realise it's not about following a bunch of rules but knowing what makes the God we love happy and longing to please Him.

When these young people who buried their drugs told me their story, I asked them what had made them decide to follow Jesus. 'Was it the humorous teaching?' I asked. 'The story I told about the chocolate cake – that was a good one, wasn't it? The eloquence of the way I delivered the message? The intellectual way I opened up the Bible?' They shook their heads more violently than I would have liked. 'It was the worship,' they responded. 'We never thought we could know God like this.'

True worship brings us closer to the heart of God, which is why from the creation of mankind He laid it at the very foundation of our life with Him. Once we've grasped the truth that God longs for our worship before anything else, and understand why, we long to give Him what He desires. What we need to know now is what that worship might look like.

2

The Worship God Requires

Over the years we have seen many worship wars in the church. We've argued over traditional or modern, organ or guitar, louder or quieter, intimacy or celebration, this worship leader or that one. Mostly, if we're honest, it's about our preferences and prejudices. The main question we should be asking is, 'What kind of worship does God require?' So, back to the Bible!

The easiest way to get an idea of the worship in the Old Testament is to take a look at the Psalms, which could be called the hymn and prayer book of Israel. Written by a number of authors, they are the expression not just of King David's worship, but all of God's people at the time.

Psalms of total honesty

If you go back and look at the Psalms again through the eyes of a worshipper you might be taken aback by one distinguishing feature displayed there: complete and utter honesty. The psalmist holds nothing back in expressing to God what's going on in his head and heart. The words spill forth in expressions of praise, songs of victory and proclamations of God's goodness and faithfulness, but the striking thing is that this is all interwoven with songs of lament and exile, expressions of pain and confusion, alongside confession of sin.

Some of the Psalms could almost be mistaken as the private prayer journal entries of someone who suffered from extreme mood swings, soaring from the highest heights of knowing God's intimate presence and mighty power then crashing to the depths of despair at times when they felt as if they'd been abandoned and forsaken by the Almighty. To be honest, if I'd written them there would be some I wouldn't have wanted to see the light of day in case people thought my faith was weak, but these no-holds-barred Psalms are included in the Bible for all to see, to show us what it means to have an intimate relationship with God.

It seems that God wasn't embarrassed by David and the other writers pouring out their hearts in the Psalms. There's no sense of Him saying, 'Oops, sorry about David – he was having a bad day, but it's OK, he's over it now. He was over-tired and a bit emotional, that's all. Of course I hadn't left him or forgotten him. He knows it was foolish talk, so we'll just edit those bits out to save him from embarrassment. Why don't we substitute the line where he says "You have put me in the lowest pit, in the darkest depths" (Psalm 88:6) with the one where he says, "You are mighty, O Lord, and your faithfulness surrounds you" (Psalm 89:8)? After all, the high points are far more encouraging for others.'

Too often we don't know how to handle people's cries to God. We worry they're not being reverent and therefore offending God with their questions, but the Psalms make it pretty clear that God wants us to pour it all out to Him – every emotion.

Jesus didn't have much time for people who were so busy putting on a show of holiness that they were forgetting to get their hearts right before His Father. In John 4:23–34 we see Jesus meet a Samaritan woman at Jacob's well and He tells her, 'True worshippers will worship the Father in spirit and truth, for they are the kind of worshippers the Father seeks.'

The amazing safety of our relationship with God is that we can tell Him anything and everything and He's not surprised – our sin, fear and doubt aren't hidden, however much we try and bury them within ourselves. God is not like a human who will respond from a place of hurt or confusion, but He does require openness and honesty if we want to have a truly intimate relationship with Him. We belittle God when we think He can't handle our emotions and questions. The Psalms, along with the book of Job, in particular illustrate that it's OK for us to question and be real about what we're going through. Honesty is what He requires. If it's going through our heads and our hearts, let's bring it before our Father.

Sometimes I think we worry about God's reputation as though by expressing pain we're letting Him down and making people think He's not all that He is. But God doesn't justify Himself by telling us what was going on behind the scenes and adding in footnotes to the Psalms. His greatness and goodness are fact, but that doesn't mean we have no struggles in life.

Songs of lament

A few years ago Matt Redman and I went to see Graham Cray, who was then the principal of a vicar factory (aka theological college) in Cambridge, as well as being a theological genius. It was one of our regular visits where we would just double-check our theology and make sure we weren't inadvertently committing heresy. We chatted pleasantly until I asked him where he thought we were going wrong. I was prepared for many of the questions that could have been thrown my way, but what Graham asked was something that God had been stirring in his own heart: 'Where is the place of lament in our worship songs?' I wondered what he was talking about. 'The songs of exile and brokenness?' he continued. 'By the rivers of Babylon we sat down and wept when we remembered Zion,' Graham quoted.

Thankfully I kept my mouth shut just long enough to remember this was written in the Psalms long before Boney M turned it into a song. Still, 'Poor Graham,' I thought. 'He just doesn't get it. He's spent too much time in Bible college and can't see the theological wood for the trees.' With my most patronising smile I reassured him, 'We're not in exile any more, Graham. When Jesus died on the cross He brought us home. We don't need to lament, only praise.'

I sat back, waiting for him to thank me for my theological insight and then I saw the look on his face. 'Who on earth told you that?' he asked. 'Is this world really home? Are we not strangers in a foreign land? Yes, Jesus broke the power of sin on the cross and restored our relationship with God. Yes, the kingdom has come now. But in another sense it is not yet in its fullness. The lion does not yet lie down with the lamb. Surely there's still a place for lament over our sin, and just because we've become Christians doesn't mean we're immune to pain in our own lives. Quite aside from us, what about the rest of the world and all the people in desperate pain and need because of war, diseases like AIDS and natural disasters? Isn't there some room in our worship to cry out for those situations?'

In the days, weeks and months that I thought about this issue after speaking to Graham, I began to realise what we've so often missed. We've focused on the joyful bits of praise, on the happy songs that express delight at being in relationship with Jesus, exalting God for all He is and does. While this joyful praise is completely fitting and right, it only tells part of the story. It is estimated that 70 per cent of the Psalms are actually songs of lament rather than rejoicing. Of course we should spend much of our worship in praise and thanksgiving because God is good all the time and He is above the circumstances; we adore Him even when life hurts. Yet the Psalms teach us we can express the hurts of life, cry out to God in intercession and still adore Him. Worship was never meant to be an escape from reality, but praising His name in the midst of real pain in a real world is real worship.

The balance between honesty and truth

Worship is a place where we can bring all our pain to God, but sometimes in our desire to hold on to the truth, we have sacrificed something of our honesty. We must of course be careful and not make the opposite error where we wallow in self-indulgent pity in the name of honesty. But we must look to strike a balance. The Psalms incorporate honesty about where the psalmist is, as well as the truth about who God is, and we must look to do the same in our worship.

One recent song that undoubtedly models the effective blending of praise and sorrow was written by Tim Hughes and is called 'When the tears fall'.

> I've had questions, without answers,
> I've known sorrow, I have known pain.

But there's one thing that I'll cling to,
You are faithful, Jesus You're true.

When hope is lost, I'll call You Saviour,
When pain surrounds, I'll call You healer,
When silence falls, You'll be the song within my heart.

In the lone hour of my sorrow,
Through the darkest night of my soul,
You surround me and sustain me,
My defender forever more.

I will praise You, I will praise You,
When the tears fall, still I will sing to You,
I will praise You, Jesus praise You,
Through the suffering still I will sing.[1]

The great thing about this song is that Tim is not denying the pain that he's experiencing, and he expresses that while holding to the truth that God is good and faithful whether Tim feels it or not. He acknowledges that even in the 'darkest night of the soul' God is right there with him in the midst of the pain, not waiting for him to get back to a happy place to come and sing a joyful song. I love the line 'When hope is lost, I'll call You Saviour'. We still praise Him as Saviour even while we mourn and grieve. To sing to God as the tears fall is true spiritual maturity; to pretend there are no tears, or worse there *should* be no tears, is naïve.

I know that sometimes my worship feels the most meaningful when I bring my pain to Jesus. I pour out my heart, tell Him

---

[1] Extract taken from the song 'When the tears fall' by Tim Hughes, copyright © 2003 Thankyou Music. Adm. by worshiptogether.com songs excl. UK & Europe, adm. by kingswaysongs.com tym@kingsway.co.uk. Used by permission.

how much it hurts and then say in the midst of this pain, 'I will praise You.' Because in one sense it's easy to worship God when life is going our way, when God feels close, when work and relationships are all ticking along nicely, the sun's shining and the birds are singing. It can seem harder to worship when we're in great physical pain, grieving the loss of a loved one, confused about which direction our life is headed, have just had our hopes and dreams crushed or just can't seem to find God. But that's the place where we need to worship. When circumstances in our lives don't seem to back it up, we need to know the truth in our hearts that God is faithful, good, loving, kind and worthy of all our praise. Because of Jesus' death on the cross we no longer have to bring physical sacrifices to God when we worship, as He made the ultimate sacrifice, but there is still a place for sacrifice today and often for us it is here, worshipping through the tears.

We know that David and Job are the classic biblical illustrations of this. David was a 'man after God's heart' and we see something of what that heart is when we hear how David responded to tragedy. God took David's son's life after his sinful relationship with Bathsheba and when David was told his child was dead 'he went into the house of the Lord and worshipped' (2 Samuel 12:20). Job was considered 'blameless and upright' in the eyes of the Lord, but Satan tried to prove that Job only loved God because of what God had given him and not for who He is. This theory was blown out of the water when we see that in just one day Job lost his sons, daughters and livelihood and yet on hearing the news 'he fell to the ground in worship' (Job 1:20). While these are two extreme examples of worshipping through the most painful of circumstances, they demonstrate hearts that were clearly in love with the Creator and not the things He created. David and Job held the Giver and not the gifts in the highest esteem and therefore even in these excruciating circumstances were able to praise God's name and declare the truth that He is good. This is a great reminder to us that our praise does not depend on our circumstances or whether we feel like it. God is worthy yesterday, today and for ever, and absolutely nothing can change that.

If we look at Psalm 77 we see the writer was going through one of the tough times that we all experience: '"Will the Lord reject for ever? … Has God forgotten to be merciful?" . . . I will remember the deeds of the Lord; yes, I will remember your miracles of long ago. I will meditate on all your works and consider all your mighty deeds' (vv. 7, 9, 11–12). I know that when things get hard in my life I find it easy to look at the circumstances and wonder if God has forgotten me and I start to question whether He really is involved in my life, but praising Him reminds me of His goodness. As the psalmist encourages us here, calling to mind His faithful deeds of the past gives us hope for His faithfulness in the current trials we face. Thanksgiving fixes our eyes back on Him, brings to mind His nature and works, and keeps us from too much unhelpful navel-gazing.

We have to be careful, however, that worship doesn't become a quick fix, the Christian equivalent of sinking a bottle of whiskey or taking a tablet. Our consumerist culture tells us that life revolves around our pleasure and it's this attitude that has contributed to the way we often look at times of worship in music as something for us. We mustn't have a consumer attitude of, 'What can I get out of the worship? What blesses me? What gives me a quick pick-me-up?' We must remember this is about offering our hearts to God. In recent years I've heard people saying, 'I can't wait for Sunday so that I can spend some time in worship. It's been such a bad week and I need some relief.' It's great to long to praise God – although we don't have to wait until we meet as a church to do it – but we mustn't use it like a God-fix to see us through the week. Christianity is not about escapism. Worship should sharpen our awareness of the things going on in our lives and in the world as we bring them before the One who has power over them, rather than give us an hour's respite.

Israel, it seems, had no problem with bringing their cries against the evil and injustice happening to them and around them into their songs to God. Psalm 55 tells us how David cried out to the Lord when a former friend had turned against him and was leading a conspiracy against him. He said, 'Let death take my enemies by surprise, let them go down alive to the grave, for evil finds lodging among them . . . My companion attacks his friends . . . His speech is smooth as butter, yet war is in his heart; his words are more soothing than oil, yet they are drawn swords' (vv. 15, 20–21).

We've often thought that anger is a sin, and that's true when we get angry about things we shouldn't. Many times in the Bible God's anger burns because His people are not doing as He has commanded them. We too should have a righteous anger about some of the terrible situations that are going on in the world right now. Worship and intercession often go hand in hand as we allow God to break our hearts with the things that break His and we in turn bring the cries back to His throne room. Or, as in this psalm, David is expressing his anger at the betrayal of his friend. He feels it so strongly he prays that his enemies would die, but he is quick to say, 'Cast your cares on the Lord and he will sustain you' (v. 22).

Rather than keeping hold of his anger or laying into someone else, he chooses to let it out before God and then to trust that God is capable of bringing about the appropriate justice. We shouldn't use times of worship to stir up anger, but rather to sit and pour it out to God before we turn again to face our troubled world.

Worship that acknowledges that we love God in a place and from a place of pain is a worship that will speak with integrity to a broken and hurting world.

The worship of heaven – Revelation 4–5

Ultimately if we want to know what our worship should look like, sound like and be like, we would do well to catch a glimpse of the worship of heaven. In Revelation chapters 4 and 5 God, through the apostle John, gives us such a glimpse. Let us look at these verses section by section and see what they show us.

> At once I was in the Spirit, and there before me was a throne in heaven with someone sitting on it. And the one who sat there had the appearance of jasper and carnelian. A rainbow, resembling an emerald, encircled the throne. (4:2–3)

So the first thing we see is a throne with someone sitting on it. I'm sure a great theologian could tell you the symbolic significance of the jasper and carnelian, but my intellectual assessment would be that they are very colourful. My insight is astounding at times, I know. But anyway, add to that an emerald rainbow and we're starting to build a very vibrant picture.

> Surrounding the throne were twenty-four other thrones, and seated on them were twenty-four elders. They were dressed in white and had crowns of gold on their heads. (4:4)

You may not be able to imagine it if you've seen the suave and sophisticated way I dress, but believe it or not I owe my dashing dress sense to some wise words from friends. You see, I used to have a habit of not really looking at what I was putting on in the morning. I'd get up, find any pair of trousers that was clean, pick one of my fantastically colourful shirts and that would be pretty much all the thought that went into my dressing routine. One morning when I was out in California with my friends Matt and Beth, I knew I was in trouble when Beth sent Matt over to talk to me. The thing is, I'd put on one of my favourite shirts with a pair of Bermuda shorts that were equally brightly patterned. The words delivered were gentle but made a significant point. 'Mike,' he said, 'when you're thinking about what to wear, why don't you try and remember a little rule of Beth's? If you want to wear a snazzy top, then wear it with plain trousers. If you want to wear a pair of trousers that have a pattern, then wear them with a simple top. To be honest, if you wanted to just wear a plain top and plain trousers that would be fine too. But please, for all our sakes, don't wear a snazzy top with snazzy trousers!'

I've taken these words to heart and so when I looked in Revelation I was pleased to see that the 24 elders also seemed to be on the same wavelength as Beth when it came to dressing. They wore plain white robes, which meant all the attention could be focused on their magnificent, brightly shining gold crowns.

> From the throne came flashes of lightning, rumblings and peals of thunder. Before the throne, seven lamps were blazing. These are the seven spirits of God. Also before the throne there was what looked like a sea of glass, clear as crystal. (4:5–6)

So in addition to the colour we now get the light and sound show, and I would hazard a guess that this was LOUD; after all, we *are* talking thunder! And the lights are not just pretty candles flickering or fairy lights twinkling; these are blazing with huge flames which add to the colour and majesty of the picture. And all of these things are reflected in the mirror of the sea of glass, just to make sure there's an extra wow factor. What does this tell us? That if there's one thing we'd better not forget to pack when we go to heaven, it's our sunglasses!

John goes on to describe the uniqueness of the four living creatures, one like a lion, the second like an ox, another like a man and the other like an eagle. And then we get to the song:

> Day and night they never stop saying: 'Holy, holy, holy is the Lord God Almighty, who was, and is, and is to come.' (4:8)

Do you realise that means that this phrase is for ever being repeated? All the time. No break. No change in wording. They gave the chorus a few minutes ago and by the time you finish reading this line they'll be doing it all over again. And of course it doesn't end there.

> Whenever the living creatures give glory, honour and thanks to him who sits on the throne and who lives for ever and ever, the twenty-four elders fall down before him who sits on the throne, and worship him who lives for ever and ever. They lay their crowns before the throne and say: 'You are worthy, our Lord and God, to receive glory and honour and power, for you created all things, and by your will they were created and have their being.' (4:9–11)

Every time the four living creatures have finished doing their 'holy, holy, holy' bit they step back and the 24 old guys take their turn. They get off their thrones, fall down on their faces, cast their crowns in front of the big throne and deliver their words of praise.

Then when they've done that the four living creatures repeat their 'holy, holy, holy' lines, during which the elders put their crowns back on and get back on the thrones so they are ready to jump off and throw down their crowns again on cue. The same thing gets repeated over and over and over again. I'm sure it's not the only thing that disqualifies me but I know I'm nowhere near fit enough to be one of the 24 elders.

> Then I looked and heard the voice of many angels, numbering thousands upon thousands, and ten thousand times ten thousand. They encircled the throne and the living creatures and the elders. In a loud voice they sang: 'Worthy is the Lamb, who was slain, to receive power and wealth and wisdom and strength and honour and glory and praise!' (5:11–12)

So what about us? Where do we come in?

> Then I heard every creature in heaven and on earth and under the earth and on the sea, and all that is in them, singing: 'To him who sits on the throne and to the Lamb be praise and honour and glory and power, for ever and ever!' (5:13)

We're the creatures on earth and we join in with the animals of the air, earth and sea to sing God's praise. Then, and I love this:

> The four living creatures said, 'Amen!' (5:14)

After all the colour and light and noise of what we've just seen, this is something of an anticlimax! But it's all it takes to set those Duracell-powered elders off again and they fall down and worship.

The heart of worship

What a picture! How breathtaking and awe-inspiring is the worship of heaven – full of colour and creativity, sound and light, praise and adoration! But if we leave it there we miss something out. And not just a little something either. Right in the middle we read that there was a scroll with seven seals, and an angel proclaimed in a loud voice:

> 'Who is worthy to break the seals and open the scroll?' But no-one in heaven or on earth or under the earth could open the scroll or even look inside it. I wept and wept because no-one was found who was worthy to open the scroll or look inside. Then one of the elders said to me, 'Do not weep! See, the Lion of the tribe of Judah, the Root of David, has triumphed.' (5:2–5)

You see, all of the other stuff we've been looking at is just the warm-up act, merely a side show to the main event. While the crowns are being thrown and the lightning is flashing, John introduces us to the star of the show, the One we've been waiting for. The thunder rumbles as the curtains open and all the creatures on heaven and earth let out a gasp at what they see: a lamb.

> Then I saw a Lamb, looking as if it had been slain, standing in the centre of the throne, encircled by the four living creatures and the elders. (5:6)

This is Jesus. All the loud noise, fireworks, clapping and cheering and jumping around, all of it is for the One who is the Lion of the tribe of Judah. And this mighty Lion, this all-conquering Saviour, appears as a lamb that's been slain. Just as God's people often used lambs as offerings of worship to atone for their sin, God Himself provides His only Son as the sacrificial Lamb that defeats sin for ever. He is at the centre of it all.

If Jesus is at the centre of the worship of heaven, He must be at the centre of the worship on earth. So you see it's really not about who leads worship, whether the lights are bright and flashing or turned down low, whether the lead guitarist has been playing for ten years or ten days or whether you stand near the front or the back of church. We may never have seven blazing lamps or a sea of crystal-clear glass and we may have more than 24 old guys trying to get in on the act, but it's not about that. It's about Him because He is so magnificent. He is awesome and wonderful, the King of kings and Lord of lords, but He will appear to us as a lamb that was slain because the King of the universe, through whom all things were created, shed His blood on a wooden cross and died for us. And that should always be at the heart of our worship.

Because He is amazing we give ourselves in worship, not just in words and song but in our hearts. When we come before Him we realise afresh that we should hold nothing back, as He is worthy of it all. Even offering up our lives seems like nothing in comparison to His glory. Our worship must go far beyond the music; it must infuse every area of our lives.

3

Worship as a Lifestyle

Society has been telling us for years that the way to contentment is having all of our desires fulfilled as quickly as possible. We're bombarded with messages about how to make our lives more comfortable and they all revolve around having our every whim realised. Strangely, no one seems to be getting any happier; they just spend more time chasing the things they want or they think they want. To be honest, even for those of us who try to live against this culture, our natural default setting seems to be that we think the world does, or at the very least *should*, revolve around us. We get caught up in our decisions, our problems, our pains, our hopes, our dreams, when really it's not about us at all. Our prayers become insular and demanding – why hasn't God given me a girlfriend? Why didn't my exams go as well as I'd hoped? What about my dreams, my desires, my heart? Me, me, me. As we worship, our focus shifts: when we put Jesus at the centre of our lives in the knowledge of all that was given for us, we humbly remember it's all about Him. When we fully catch this glimpse of His worth we offer our lives gladly, but what does that look like?

Worship leader David Ruis wrote this in his book *The Worship*

God Is Seeking: 'The only true expression of worship is through the abandonment of all our agendas for His, as we trust in His sovereign power and unlimited grace' (p.12). Worship, it seems, is about surrendering all areas of our lives to God, giving our hearts, our careers, our money, our time and everything else at our disposal to serve Him; in all areas of our lives choosing to echo Jesus' words before He went to the cross, saying, 'Not my will but Yours be done.'   These may be some of the hardest words to pray as we bring our hopes, dreams and fears to God. It costs to abandon our own agendas in favour of His, but there is no safer or more rewarding place to be.

The offering of our lives

Somehow over the years we've created a hierarchy of holiness within the church when it comes to employment. At the very top, with the ultimate way to love and serve God, are the worship leaders and big-stage evangelists. Following hot on their heels for the second seat at the table of holiness are the overseas missionaries. And of course God clearly uses those who work full time for the church, so they happily slide into third place. At number four are the 'worthy secular jobs', so we're talking about doctors, nurses, teachers and generally those who get paid to help others. Languishing at the bottom of the table, not valued by us and we suppose by God, are those of us who do 'normal jobs'. If you're a plumber, a secretary, an accountant or a builder, how can God possibly use you in your work? Of course the money you earn is brought back into the church, so that's of some value, but the way you get it? Who cares?

Let me tell you about a poor fool who thought just that way. He became a Christian at the age of 16 and with a heart desperate to serve God and a passion to preach His word, decided that no other job would be good enough than to work full time within the church. His name? Mike Pilavachi. It makes me cringe to think about it now, but I became an accountant to pass the time until the call to Africa came or the worldwide Mike Pilavachi preaching roadshow took off. I spent the next twelve years – twelve years! – asking God to rescue me. I yearned so much for Him to use me and yet missed opportunities daily for Him to do just that. I was so focused on what was in the future I couldn't see what was right in front of me. It dawned on me slowly, and I do mean slowly, that God wanted me to be satisfied serving Him in my job whatever I was doing; that to Him, worship and service meant to go where He called me and to do the things in front of me well and to His glory.

As Paul wrote to the Colossians, 'Whatever you do, work at it with all your heart, as working for the Lord, not for men, since you know that you will receive an inheritance from the Lord as a reward. It is the Lord Christ you are serving' (Colossians 3:23–24). The irony is, it was only as I began to see the truth that being a full time Christian worker simply meant doing my work with a heart of thankfulness and worship to God, and so began to appreciate the opportunities I'd been given where I was, that He opened the door to something else.

Although I regret the way I handled my time as an account-ant, I'm so thankful to God for teaching me such a valuable les-son. If He'd moved me on any sooner I would have thought that those were wasted years until I started my ministry. 'Ministry' is a much misused word in the church today – being an account-ant was as much my ministry as working as a youth leader. There is no hierarchy in God's eyes; He doesn't find one gift more useful than another. You don't serve Him more by leading worship at church than by pouring tea and coffee in a café; by speaking to a congregation of hundreds than by chatting to the person at the desk next to you. Everything we do, if offered to our heavenly Father and done in love, is an act of worship.

The division of sacred and secular

We need to reclaim the truth that nothing is secular and everything is sacred for the Christian who wants to truly worship God with their life. In Hebrew culture they didn't divide the sacred and secular as we do. This is so clear when you read the law of Moses; there's stuff about what to do in the temple and then on the next page there are instructions about how to handle your cattle, how to treat your wife and neighbours, what to do with your money and your tithe. It's all in there together and we've lost how intensely practical the Bible is and how God is interested in and involved in all aspects of our lives.

One of the most inspirational books I've ever read was written by a seventeenth-century French monk called Brother Lawrence. Desperate to live in constant communion with God, he chose to become a monk and learned to practise the presence of God whatever he was doing. The many hours he spent in the kitchen washing dishes were not wasted in his eyes, but 'having taken as the end of all his actions, to do them all for the love of God, he was satisfied therewith' (*The Practice of the Presence of God* , p. 21). He learned that we can invite God's presence into all areas of our lives; that true happiness comes from doing all things as an act of worship to Him, and making everything we do about Him.

Because these opportunities to worship are disguised as normal parts of everyday life, they are easy to miss. A few years ago

Tim Hughes and I were in Port Elizabeth, South Africa, where we were invited to go to a Christian radio station and talk about worship. We enjoyed chatting with the host about many different aspects of worship and the novelty of acting like experts. As we left the building and were about to get into our car, two small children came up to us. They wore ragged clothes and their faces were dirty; it was obvious they were two of the many street children in that area. They came over and begged us for some money. I patted my pockets and apologised: 'I'm sorry; I don't have any change. I don't have anything to give you.' We climbed into our car and watched them walk away empty-handed. Two seconds later it hit me like a tonne of bricks what had just happened: God, having given me an opportunity to talk about worship, had just given me an opportunity to express an act of worship, and I'd totally missed it. My heart pounded until we stopped at some lights and saw them again. Beckoning them over I pulled out a 50-rand note and pressed it into their hands. Their faces lit up immediately, as though I had handed them a fortune (the equivalent in Britain might be about £3). 'Do you know where this comes from?' I asked them. 'Yes sir,' they replied immediately. 'From Jesus.' There was no prompting and I guess they knew the truth that in myself I wasn't quick enough to give, but Jesus living in me was the One who prompted me to hand over the money. They ran off jumping for joy and I thanked God that He had given me a second chance to literally put my money where my mouth was. I almost missed an opportunity to demonstrate the very thing I had just been so happy to talk about: worship. Giving to those boys was first and foremost an act of love from me to my Saviour.

If we want better worship on a Sunday then the answer probably doesn't lie in changing the order of the songs or getting a new guitarist. We gather at church and worship with our words and our voices, and then we should be spending the rest of the week acting out that worship in all sorts of ways, from how we love and care for our friends and families, to what we do with our money, how we carry out our work tasks and how we treat those with less than we have. If our lives don't match up to our songs, the words become meaningless; but when they do, our praises in church are richer, as they come from the overflow of hearts that have spent the entire week praising God. The music is an act of worship, but for this worship to be genuine it has to be connected to and demonstrated throughout all areas of our lives.

As we do this we find that the happiness and satisfaction that the world tells us is achievable is not realised through owning the coolest clothes, going on better holidays or seeing our every dream come true. It's not even, as some of us in the church have believed, through serving the Lord by becoming a worship leader or a missionary. It's looking for ways every day to love and bless God, however simple they may be and however over-looked by others, and realising that God not only sees but accepts each one as an act of devotion.

For us to respond to people and their needs in this world as Jesus would, we need God to change our hearts to make them more like His. Amazing things happen when we worship; as we spend more time with Jesus, we begin to care about the things He cares about. Richard Foster sums it up so simply when he says in his *Celebration of Discipline*: 'To worship is to change.'

I'd say it was impossible to connect with God as we do in intimate times of worship and to leave the same. Our hearts get stretched and challenged, and we begin to long to take all that we've found in Him out onto the streets, away from the safety of the church and to a world that needs to know its Saviour. The more we see of Him, the more we want others to know about Him; it's a natural reaction when you fall in love – you want to tell people about the wonderful person you have given your heart to. It should be this infectious enthusiasm, this burning love for Jesus and sharing in His heart for the world, that propels us from the pews to the people outside of the church.

Part 2

EVANGELISM

4
Why Evangelise?

In recent years people have written God and the church off as irrelevant and boring – outdated and bearing no relation to their lives. We in the church have been very good at telling people what we're against – to the point that they often have no idea what being a Christian means beyond not smoking, drinking, swearing or having sex before marriage. We've signed petitions and pointed our finger at lifestyles we don't approve of and in so doing we've made enemies of the people who don't live life the way we do. Of course it's vitally important that we stand up for righteousness and don't water down biblical truths to fit in with society, but we seem to have so poorly represented Jesus that most people couldn't tell you what He is *for*.

If we want to better represent Jesus then we'd be wise to remember some of His characteristics. From the Bible, but also from our own lives, we know that Jesus is loving, compassionate, full of grace and mercy, kind, humble, forgiving and passionate. Would those outside of the church say the same about us?

A few years ago I visited a church in America where there was a notice displayed asking people not to use the petrol station next door. Curiosity getting the better of me I asked why, intrigued at what would stop everyone from using the facility. I was shocked by the answer. 'It's run by Muslims,' came the response, as though that was a reason in itself. Nothing spoke to me more gravely of the way we have built up an idea of it being 'them versus us', with us in the safety of the church and them as the big bad world outside.

How on earth do we expect people to get to know the living God if we, as God's representatives on earth, behave like that? How we treat them reflects how we think God feels about them, so what does it tell them when we boycott their business and try to ruin their livelihood? Shouldn't we be doing the opposite? Rather than being a destructive influence in someone's life because we don't agree with their beliefs, we should be blessing them and supporting them. What would have happened if that church had decided to get involved with the people running that petrol station? If they had committed to praying for them? Chosen to get involved and love and bless them rather than showing them a cold shoulder? What would speak more of the love and compassion of Jesus?

What's the best way to tell people about Jesus?

'Evangelism' has become a word that for many of us is loaded with guilt and confusion. It seems as if the church has always known it needs to tell the rest of the world about Jesus, but we've never been quite sure of how to go about doing it. So we've come up with strategies, theories and templates in the hope of drawing people into the church that have sadly left many of us floundering.

Few Christians would doubt Jesus' intention when He left us

with the Great Commission to 'go and make disciples of all nations', but many would argue over the best way to go about it. Each group, having taken a good long look at how Jesus did things in the Bible, has put its own spin on things.

For some of us it's been 'proclamation evangelism'. Those of us who fall into this camp have believed that the best way to communicate Jesus is through direct words. We can take the words of Mark 16 to 'preach the good news' as a literal translation of 'preach', which means 'to speak earnestly', and follow the logic that Jesus preached publicly and many people were saved, so it must be about the words.

Others of us would say that it's not so much about what we say but the way we live our lives. There is a world around us full of broken and hurting people. Human beings made in God's image are daily living without even the basics of food and shelter, so there are plenty of needs we can meet in the name of Jesus. Those of us who believe this is the best method of evangelism use the words of St Francis of Assisi, who famously said, 'Preach the gospel at all times and when necessary use words.' This is certainly in line with the fact that when we look at Jesus we see it was often the things He did as well as the things He said that captured people's attention and brought them to faith, so maybe 'works' is the way forward.

But there has also been yet another school of thought where it is said that it was the signs and wonders Jesus did that really opened people's hearts to the gospel. And we do see in the Gospels and the book of Acts how the blind received their sight, the sick were healed and the dead were raised to life, and as a result many people put their faith in Jesus.

So which is right? Well, these methods of evangelism are all rooted in Scripture and our understanding of how Jesus lived

His life, so I would suggest that they are *all* right. The best way to communicate Jesus is with all the tools at our disposal: words, works *and* wonders. If people see Jesus in our actions but don't hear our words then how will they know their own need for a Saviour or understand what it means to be in relationship with Him? And surely we're shooting ourselves in the foot if we tell people about Jesus, but they don't see us putting His words into action in our own lives. On top of this there's a hunger and passion for the supernatural inside us – part of the deep call in our spirits to know that there is more to life than what we can hear, see, touch, smell and taste. When people see miracles and healings they see something of the power of God that is hard to argue with.

Throughout His ministry Jesus set out plain truths in His preaching, He cared for the poor and the marginalised and He cast out demons and healed the sick. If we use Jesus as our model for effective evangelism then we can't deny the power to reach people when all these elements are used together.

But even when we see that, evangelism still feels like something of a scary concept. If someone mentions the word 'evangelism', we start to look guilty, we don't know where to start or we look back at times we've got ourselves all excited about evangelism and then the mission we poured our hearts into yielded little result.

Sometimes it feels as if we've decided the only place we are safe from the contamination of the world is behind walls. We've tried to make the church like a safe castle where we live apart from the rest of the world so that they can't get us. Every now and then we feel guilty because we know Jesus called us to make disciples of all nations, so we 'do a mission'. We practise our Christian plays and testimonies, let down the drawbridge, run out of the castle, 'do some evangelism' and hope to take some captives (by force if necessary) to bring back with us. If by any chance we do get someone to follow us back, we do something to them that we've called 'discipleship' but really seems to involve making them clones of us so that they too can't relate to anyone outside of the safety of the church. We've called this process evangelism, but really it's anti-evangelism. We're not called to live apart from the world and only come out once or twice a year; we're called to live without walls, to be an active part of our community and to influence it for Jesus.

One of the saddest things I've seen was a group of young people at a Christian conference, many of whom had just given their lives to God. These people were passionate for Jesus; they'd met Him and fallen in love and were in the process of working out how to live their lives for Him. So far so encouraging – how amazing to see God transforming people's lives. The thing that broke my heart was what they were then taught. The preacher got a young lad from the crowd and got him to stand on a chair in front of everyone. 'Try and pull me up,' she said, offering him her hand. He gave it his best shot, but for little reward; there was no moving her from the ground. 'Now let me see if I can pull you down,' she continued, and with one tug that was it – he fell from the chair. I was horrified by the point she was making – that as a Christian you can't influence others to get to know Jesus, but they will pull you away. I couldn't believe that these young people were being told that if they wanted to live holy lives they needed to stop seeing their friends who didn't know Jesus.

We've so often believed that if we keep hanging out with people outside of the church we will be contaminated and polluted by the world. But that's the extreme opposite of the example that Jesus set for us because He hung out with the worst of sinners. And it wasn't by accident or because there was no one else to talk to. He actively sought out the people who were considered the furthest from God (the thieves, the prostitutes, the drunks) and chose to spend time with them. In fact He spent so much time with them that people accused Him of being like them and being a drunkard and a glutton.

The Pharisees had built their lives on trying to follow the word of God and to keep themselves pure and holy as He intended them to be. There were many laws concerning keeping yourself ceremonially clean that they followed strictly. Sadly, in their desire to stay clean they began to take things much further than God required, to the point where they would have been offended to see Jesus hang out with those they considered unholy. In this and in many other ways, Jesus came to show that the compassion of God stretched far beyond a list of rules. He didn't seem to care in the slightest about being friends with those who weren't acceptable in 'polite society'. He wasn't bothered about His reputation because that wasn't His identity or His motivation and He knew that the people He was reaching would otherwise go unnoticed by the religious leaders. Can we say the same? That we are happy to hang out with the people society would tell us are the lowest and the least – those who will never be a part of the 'in crowd'? If people judge and misunderstand us, will we be OK with that and know that no one has a higher or lower place in God's eyes?

So if Jesus wasn't interested in building up a good reputation for Himself, what was His motivation for hanging out with sinners? This is a key point for us, which we're going to look at in more detail in the next chapter, as our motivation needs to be the same as His.

to wander off and get lost themselves. So when Jesus told this story, everyone listening would have thought, 'What a weird shepherd. He's rejoicing because he found the one sheep that he lost, but he must be *really* stupid not to realise that he lost 99 to do it.' Then Jesus hits them with the punchline: God is like that shepherd.

The point of the story that I had so often missed is not that God doesn't protect His own, but that He sees individuals. He wants to be involved, to have them know the intimate care with which He looks over them. Each individual person matters to Him and that's the main point of the parable.

Jesus had a strategy, but it wasn't motivated by a need to speak to big crowds or to get His message as far and wide as possible. His strategy was to love. He cared for and had compassion on individuals. Now that's a strategy worth making our own.

Of course we pray and long for lots of people to know Jesus, but rather than seeing a mass of people waiting to be converted we need to see with Jesus' eyes; to see people one at a time and their own particular needs.

Many times we read in the Gospels that Jesus had compassion on people, but we don't always take in fully what was meant by that. The Greek word for compassion that Jesus used literally meant a 'tearing of the gut'.

One such time was when Jesus met a man who had leprosy, which we read about in Mark 1:40–45. It is likely this man was not only suffering from his physical ailments but from the emotional pain of being cast out from society, as people with leprosy in those days were forced to announce their presence everywhere they went to allow people time to get away from them. But he dared to come close to Jesus, kneel before Him and make his request to be made clean. Jesus didn't recoil in horror, as people at the time would have done when so close to a person with leprosy. Instead, 'Filled with compassion, Jesus reached out his hand and touched the man. "I am willing," he said. "Be clean!"' (v. 41).

What I love about this is that Jesus not only healed the man's physical condition as He was asked, but He must have restored so much more in the man's heart. Jesus would probably have been the first person to touch him in years and He did it from a place of love and desire for the man to be whole.

Jesus' concern was often very practical too. The feeding of the four thousand took place after He said, 'I have compassion for these people; they have already been with me three days and have nothing to eat' (Mark 8:2).

Of course spiritual need touched Jesus deeply. *The Message* tells us that when Jesus saw a crowd 'his heart broke – like sheep with no shepherd they were. He went right to work teaching them' (Mark 6:34). Jesus never patronised or looked down on people, but responded to them from a place of genuine compassion and love.

Loving sinners

We live in a world full of lonely and hurting people, in an age where hope often seems hard to come by and where one of our favourite phrases is 'You don't get something for nothing'. We need to meet people's needs, to get to know them, to love them, to see them just as Jesus saw Zacchaeus and the man with leprosy. We need to care for individuals not because we want to rack up the numbers of people on our evangelism quota but because we love them. We need to share God's heart for

6

From Water to Worship

How not to do it

When I was at university I was very proud of the label I was given by my fellow students: 'God Squad'. I thought it meant I was doing a fantastic job of preaching about Jesus, whereas I think that really I was just putting people off. I had a strategy of my very own that I would employ every lunchtime, and there was a booklet based on the Four Spiritual Laws that I used as my weapon of choice. It's worth noting here that the booklet itself was actually a great resource, but my use of it could be considered more of an abuse. I would stake out the campus canteen and look for a poor unsuspecting person to be my victim. I had finely tuned senses, like a lion that spots a buffalo straying from the safety of the herd and knows exactly when to pounce. Sitting down opposite this unfortunate person I would grin from ear to ear and wait. They would look up and I'd grin. They'd look down and I'd still be grinning. Sure enough they'd look up again, wondering why I hadn't gone away, and still I would smile until they were completely unnerved. Then I'd introduce myself and ask their name. When they replied I said, 'Good to meet you [insert name of random stranger]. Have you thought about your eternal destiny?' During the next few moments, where they looked both confused and somewhat frightened, I would wade in with diagrams and illustrations from the spiritual laws booklet and explain their need for a Saviour. 'Where do you think you are on this path?' I would ask before offering to pray for them to know Jesus. It still amazes me that a number of them said that I could pray for them, but the thing was, I never saw those people again. They avoided me, as I was a religious nut who had no idea how to relate to them and so they had no idea how to relate to me.

From water to worship

After that frightening model of how *not* to evangelise, let's have a look at how Jesus did it and get to grips with some practicalities of evangelism that might make it less scary for us all. A great example of what Jesus did can be seen in John 4. We see that Jesus is walking through Samaria and, tired from His journey, He stops by a well to rest: 'When a Samaritan woman came to draw water, Jesus said to her, "Will you give me a drink?"' (v. 7).

To anyone of the day there would be many things wrong with this picture. Jesus was breaking all cultural and social boundaries by talking to her; to start with there was the fact that she was a woman, and devout Jews of Jesus' day would not have begun a private conversation with a woman. Secondly, she was a Samaritan. We tend to associate the word 'good' with Samaritan these days, so let us not forget that things would have been very different then, as the Samaritans were not a popular bunch. And as if these two things weren't bad enough, it's easy to tell this woman was considered a very bad character and an outcast from respectable society. All the women drew water during the cool of the early morning or evening, but here she was, alone, getting water in the heat of the day, probably so she could avoid the other women, who knew her reputation and wouldn't want to be seen with her.

Jesus engages her in conversation. A good point to note here with regard to striking up a conversation with someone about Jesus is start where they are at. Jesus didn't wade in with an explanation about who He was or why He had to come to earth to live and die and reconcile us to God; He started with talking about the water she was there to draw from the well. Put simply: 'Will you give Me a drink?' This confused the woman because to share a drinking cup with her would have made Jesus ceremonially unclean.

Then Jesus confuses her further: 'If you knew the gift of God and who it is that asks you for a drink, you would have asked him and he would have given you living water . . . whoever drinks the water I give him will never thirst' (vv. 10, 14). Eagerly the woman asks for the water that will quench her thirst and Jesus replies: 'Go, call your husband and come back' (v. 16). Here we find out what Jesus already knew: the woman had five husbands, which is a fair few more than her allotted quota. When she hears Him speaking words of truth into her life she recognises that Jesus is a prophet and so it is she who brings the subject round to worship in verse 20: 'Our fathers worshipped on this mountain, but you Jews claim that the place where we must worship is in Jerusalem.'

Using the gift of prophecy

Although Jesus had insight into her life, He didn't announce with pointed finger and raised eyebrow, 'I am the Son of God. My Father has just given Me a full update on your sexual immorality and I have a few things to say.' The gift of prophecy can be a powerful tool in our evangelism, but sometimes it feels as though we've forgotten how to use it.

A friend of mine, Blaine Cook, told me how one day he was walking through a local park during his lunch hour. He saw a woman sat on a bench and he felt God was saying to him, 'She's lonely and needs a friend. Go and talk to her about Me.' Knowing he had to respond, Blaine approached her with his heart in his mouth and asked her if she was lonely and needed a friend. Tears sprang to her eyes and she said yes. 'Can I tell you about Jesus?' he asked. With her permission he began to tell her about a Friend who could relieve her loneliness, and sure enough a few weeks later she committed her life to the Lord. Of course Blaine took a risk in trusting that he'd heard God's voice, but that risk paid off. He even asked the woman a while later, 'If I had been wrong when I sat down and asked if you were lonely, what would you have thought of me?' 'I would have thought you cared,' she replied. So often we worry we'll make mistakes and what people will think of us if we do, but maybe there's a lesson to learn here in humbly approaching people, knowing that if at worst we are wrong they will know that someone cared enough to ask.

The idea of walking up to someone you've never met and offering them a word from God can seem like a scary prospect, but it's not the only way to use the gift of prophecy in evangel-ism. With the woman at the well Jesus first says, 'Go, call your husband and come back,' which brings the subject round to what He knows about her. We can pray for our friends and see if God says anything to us, but we don't then need to announce it in 'Thus sayeth the Lord' fashion. We can just bring the conversation round to the area into which we feel God has given us insight, allow them the opportunity to open up and talk about it and maybe offer to pray for them. Sometimes when we try to explain to people who don't know God how and why we think God speaks, this can detract from them hearing what God is trying to say. Prophecy must be carefully, gently and lovingly handled so we don't cause offence, but it is a God-given tool that we shouldn't forget to use outside of the church.

Divine encounters

Was it by chance that Jesus encountered the woman at the well? Was it by chance that Blaine saw the woman during his lunch break? People often talk about 'divine appointments' (and it's not just a term my PA uses when I turn up at the right place, on the right day, at the right time). We use it to mean an encounter God has pre-planned for us, but I wonder if we would all have more divine encounters if we had our eyes open and looked for them each day. Life is busy and we tend to rush around from one thing to the next, but I believe that the more open we are, the more opportunities we will see to share God's love with people. Why not take a few minutes every now and then to look around and pray quietly for God's power and presence to fall? We often think we have to create opportunities ourselves, but the best way is to follow the lead of the Holy Spirit. When we try hard and force people to listen to us, or push tracts into their hands, it's often hard work that yields few results. We need to ask God to open doors for us rather than trying to break them down with a sledge-hammer.

How about making a habit of praying every morning and asking God, 'Who do You have for me to talk to, to love or to serve today?'? Inviting the Holy Spirit to make us aware of those who are put across our path for a reason makes us more attentive to moments we might otherwise miss. In football the best strikers are the ones who stay alert around the penalty area for the full 90 minutes of the game, so that when an opening comes they are ready to put the ball in the back of the net. There are strikers who wander around aimlessly and get out of position. When the ball comes their way they are not ready and opportunities are missed. We need to remember to be alert to possibilities, to keep our eyes open and to be ready at all times.

Notice that in the encounter with the woman at the well, although Jesus exposed her sin, He also gave her dignity: 'You are right when you say you have no husband. The fact is, you have had five husbands, and the man you now have is not your husband. What you have just said is quite true' (vv. 17–18). Though He knew that what she was doing was wrong and was ultimately causing her great pain, He didn't wade in with condemnation but spoke kindly to her and offered her something better than she already had. Again we see that Jesus' motivation was not to add another faceless person to the Book of Life but to love the individual.

Rather than hiring the local town hall for an all-trumpets-blaring crusade, Jesus chose to stay out of town for the individual and she got the honour of being the first person to testify about Him. In fact Jesus didn't need to go to the town because once the people heard about His meeting with the Samaritan woman, they came and found Him. The testimony of one who has been healed, loved and touched by Jesus is powerful.

But I'm not an evangelist. . .

Says who? When Jesus gave the Great Commission to make disciples of every people group, He didn't give anyone an exemption note. We are all God's representatives and we preach something with our lives whether we intend to or not. If you choose to stay away from non-Christians they are likely to believe that God has no interest in them. If you choose to judge they will think that God only judges them. But if you choose to love them they may just start to believe that God loves them too. We can't leave it up to the main-stage evangelists. Sure there are some people who have an amazing anointing to preach and lead people to the Lord, but if you think about the people who come to evangelistic events, where did they come from? Few wander in from the streets by chance; most are brought by friends or family members who have been loving and praying for them for years. They may make a commitment at a big event, but they would never have got there if it weren't for the other evangelists in their lives.

A few practical tips

Let's look at a few basic principles and practicalities of evangelism that might make it seem a bit less daunting. First, coming back to Jesus as our example, sometimes we forget that while being the Son of God, He also lived many elements of His life in a very normal fashion. Jesus built relationships with people, He was sociable, choosing to have dinner with those He called to follow Him, to go to parties and meet people, not staying in a holy huddle with a few 'safe' friends. The best thing we can do is follow Jesus' example; to see people as people and not as potential converts; to care for individuals and not worry about getting our numbers up.

Don't leave your personality at home

Because we are all made differently we all have different ways of communicating. In evangelism, as in any other area of our life, I believe Jesus uses who we are and the things that are natural to our personality type to communicate. If you love people and have a passion for them to know Jesus but can't bear the thought of talking to a crowd then it's unlikely God will call you to a ministry of preaching to hundreds of non-Christians. Of course that doesn't mean you're not called to be an evangelist. Some people love wading in and talking to a shop assistant about how their day is going in the hope of getting a good conversation going. If that thought makes you want to curl up into yourself and never set foot in a shop again, perhaps that's not for you, but if that excites you then make it a regular practice and pray God would give you great opportunities to speak His words in those situations.

Some of the most effective evangelists are those whose main qualification is that they are great at just being friends with people. They love people for who they are, they keep in touch and call or email regularly, they remember details about the other person's life and ask how things are going. OK, it's not rocket science, but that doesn't mean it isn't effective. Jesus wants you as you are. We've often thought that evangelism means doing things that make us cringe, but if it's making you feel like that then imagine how it's making the other person feel! Sometimes we are pushed out of our comfort zone, and that is no bad thing, but we shouldn't be making people feel awkward and forcing them into conversations that they clearly do not want to have.

Remember what your job is and what your job isn't

One of the reasons people get frustrated in life is because they set themselves goals they cannot achieve. You can't set out to 'save' somebody, as you have no power to do that. Your job is to love, and God's is to save. You can't do His job, but you do need Him to be able to do yours. What you can influence and achieve is being the best friend you can possibly be and to love and treat people how Jesus would, so make that your goal and bring it prayerfully before God.

Choosing friends

OK, I'm not really going to teach you how to make friends; I just want to remind you of what you already know. When you start to hang out with someone and find you have fun together and share similar interests (any Man United supporter is a friend to me), you work out whether this person is someone you want in your life. Easy! So when you're making friends with non-Christians the same rules apply. Love must be genuine. People can see through insincerity and nothing is more off-putting than someone who is spending time with you as a project. If you're going to be in it for the long haul (which is what we should be aiming for) you need to have friends you're happy to journey with. (That doesn't mean I'm saying we should only love people who are easy to love, as God calls us to love everyone, but here we are talking about choosing friends.)

Finding friends

Many of us already have people in our lives who don't know Jesus, whether they are friends, family, neighbours, work colleagues or fellow students. But some of us want to get to know more people or have a heart for a particular group to become Christians.

As Soul Survivor Watford we've undertaken a number of initiatives over the years in order to make genuine and lasting friendships with the young people in the area. We started off with Dreggs – a café run every Friday night with live music, a relaxed atmosphere and café-style food. As the mix of people changed and so did our facilities, we were able to turn this into a dance venue. We learned many things along the way about what worked and what didn't, but we tried to always put on events that achieved the aim of helping us build relationships with young people in the area. If the music got so loud we couldn't talk to people, we turned it down. If people weren't coming because it wasn't their thing, we tried to adapt it to attract people again. The point was to build lasting relationships and to provide somewhere that was almost a stepping-stone to going to church.

We started off by going into schools and letting them know that we were putting on a free event where they were welcome to hang out. We told them we were Christians, but promised we wouldn't preach at them. In fact I threatened the whole team that if I caught anyone bringing up Jesus before they were asked, I would personally persecute them for many years to come! We saw our role as simply that of befriending people and as we did that they really opened up and began to ask us about our faith.

One night we held a seventies disco and everyone got dressed up – sideburns, flares and all – and I saw two girls, one from the school and one from our team, wearing exactly the same outfit. Being as tactful as I am, I went up to them and said, 'That's pretty embarrassing that you're dressed the same.' 'Not at all,' replied the school girl proudly. 'We planned it.' As it turns out a member of our team had made friends with her and they'd spent the last few evenings choosing material and then making up outfits that were identical. This same girl was one of the first to become a Christian through Dreggs. Yes, it was because we told her about Jesus, but we had the right and the relationship to tell her because one of our team cared enough to spend time with her making an outfit for a disco night.

Being part of Dreggs also made the young people feel as though they had some ownership of the church meetings. When they first decided they wanted to come to church, they would walk in and see the same décor they'd seen in the café on the Friday night. 'It doesn't look like church; it looks like Dreggs,' they'd day. Then they would look and see that the same band that had been doing covers of modern songs in a café setting were now leading others in worship. They felt comfortable with us because they already had a relationship with us and knew that they belonged, which gave them a sense of ownership. What we were trying to do was to build a bridge between the church and the unchurched people in the area, to walk across the bridge to them and then walk back with them by our sides, because that's what we understand to be the principle of relational evangelism.

Be open about your faith, but don't push people

Being someone's friend means you respect their wishes just as you want them to respect yours. If you try and force-feed someone the gospel you're unlikely to win them to salvation but highly likely to make them sick and damage your friendship in the process. There's no formula of when or how to talk about Jesus. Of course it's vital that we're open about our faith, but this can come up in natural ways. For example, 'What did you do over the weekend?' is a fairly common question on a Monday morning. Mentioning that you went to church on Sunday is a non-threatening way of letting people know about your faith. If they ask more, go with it, and if they don't then leave it at that for now. Don't feel as though you have to make big announcements in a holy voice to get people's attention.

Listen

Everyone's journey is different. It's all very well you meeting a mate armed with all the answers on evolution versus creation, but if your friend wants to know about what proof we have that Jesus exists it's not much good, is it?

There are many reasons why the Alpha courses have worked so well and been so effective, and one of them is that people are given the opportunity to have their say. The idea is that they can discuss what they think rather than just sitting and being told what we in the church think. People want to be heard, and unless we listen carefully we won't fully understand where our friends and family are coming from.

Don't think people expect you to have all the answers just because you're a Christian. Why bluff your way through it rather than be honest and say, 'Do you know, I'm not sure I know enough about that to give you a good answer, but I'm really happy to find out some more for you if you'd like'? Buy them a book or a tape on tricky subjects if they're genuinely interested and don't feel as though you have to have all the answers (because let's face it, we never will). People usually respect you more for saying you're not sure than pretending to know and understand things that you don't.

Pray

This is another obvious one; but don't forget to involve God! Pray for their salvation as well as for God's hand of blessing on their lives. Sometimes it's appropriate to let someone know if you're praying for them over a particular situation and more people than you'd expect are touched by that in a positive way. Again the key thing is to handle it sensitively and be respectful of their wishes.

So maybe evangelism is not so scary after all! When we know that our basic qualification for evangelism is loving God and those who don't know Him, the idea is a lot less daunting. If we've felt disheartened that people aren't interested in God any more, then we need to remember it's not that He is outdated in today's culture but that maybe the methods we've used to communicate His message are. We don't need to set ourselves challenges that only set us up for a fall, like trying to convert whole cities in one weekend using the latest evangelism strategy. We just need to follow Jesus' example to see people as individuals, not judging them but building genuine and lasting relationships and being committed to them simply because we love them.

The question of suffering

I've often found that one of the first questions non-Christians will ask about my faith is: 'If this God of yours is so loving and powerful, why is there so much suffering in the world?'

If only there were a succinct three-point 30-second answer we could memorise to help us out of that spot! Part of the question people are asking is 'Does God care?' and we know that answer is a resounding 'Yes!' Most people may never pick up a Bible for long enough to see just how passionate God is about ending pain and suffering, so again ours may be the only voice they hear in answer to that question. The way we respond can't just be in words. We know that God could come and bring justice and remove suffering in an instant, but He chooses to use us. One of the most effective ways of letting people outside of the church see God's heart for this world is if we, His people who represent Him on this earth, go out and demonstrate it with our lives.

Part 3
JUSTICE

7

God's Heart for Justice

'Justice' seems to be a buzzword in today's culture, with pop stars and politicians alike proclaiming the needs of the world. This is great and can make a real difference, but what happens in a few years when it's no longer fashionable to be talking about it? For Christians it's not an option for justice to be in or out of style; we should be committed to it as a way of life because it is one of the key expressions of God's heart. The Bible is absolutely clear that God is passionate about how the poor, the oppressed, the marginalised and the dispossessed are treated.

> The righteous care about justice for the poor,
> but the wicked have no such concern.
> (Proverbs 29:7)

It's often been said that if God says something once in the Bible, He means it, and if He says it twice, He *really* means it. So if I tell you that this subject warrants 500 verses of direct teaching in the New Testament alone, you'd probably rub a few brain cells together and conclude that it's something that is pretty close to God's heart. In fact I'd go so far as to say He is completely and utterly passionate about it. We often worry about things like the second coming, sexual immorality and the nature of heaven and hell, but there's something else higher up God's agenda. It's how we handle our money and how we treat the poor, oppressed and marginalised. In fact the only topic that has more teachings devoted to it in the whole of the Bible is idolatry.

One in sixteen New Testament verses and one in twelve in the Gospels speak about God's passion for the poor. What does that tell us? If we were to cut out the verses of the Bible that talk about how we deal with our money and possessions in the light of the poor then all we'd be left with is a Bible full of holes. Could it be that for many years we have been ignoring this issue and preaching from the tattered remains of what is left of our Bibles? We've often got hung up on things Jesus didn't spend that much time talking about and overlooked the very heartbeat of God. Because it's not just the number of times the Bible talks about these things, it's also the passion with which God speaks about it.

Take this passage from Isaiah 58. This is one passage that doesn't need a skilled Bible teacher to bring out the meaning; it could not be more clear or obvious. The people have been complaining that they have been upholding their religious duties and yet God's ears seem to be closed to their prayers. God's response is passionate and direct, and you can find it in Isaiah 58:5–12. (I'm quoting here from the *Message* translation.)

> Do you think this is the kind of fast day I'm after:
> a day to show off humility?
> To put on a pious long face
> and parade around solemnly in black?
> Do you call *that* fasting,
> a fast day that I, God, would like?

God is angry that they spend all their time worrying about the outward appearance of righteousness with little regard for what it really means to be holy and how God wants them to act. They have separated the spiritual from the secular; they keep the law religiously, make a great show of fasting, but then exploit their workers. God doesn't leave them to second guess what's really important to Him and what He's really after. He makes it clear: you can't keep up this show of being My followers without acting on the things I am passionate about.

> This is the kind of fast day I'm after:
> to break the chains of injustice,
> get rid of exploitation in the workplace,
> free the oppressed,
> cancel debts.
> What I'm interested in seeing you do is:
> sharing your food with the hungry,
> inviting the homeless poor into your homes,
> putting clothes on the shivering ill-clad,
> being available to your own families.

These are the issues God cares about, not whether we wear black when we are fasting but whether we love Him enough to look after those in need. He wants to know that our hearts are moved by people's plight and that we follow through into action.

But, as we said earlier, as you give to God, He can't seem to help but give back to you and here He makes great promises to His people. This is an amazing example of God's grace – they were really messing up and getting it wrong, yet God was willing to make wonderful pledges of goodness to them if they would turn again to His ways. Isn't that amazing? And a good job too when I look at my own life and remember the countless times I've sung the songs but not lived the life. Thank God that we can always start over and it's never too late to try and get it right.

> Do this and the lights will turn on,
> and your lives will turn around at once.
> Your righteousness will pave your way.
> The God of glory will secure your passage.
> Then when you pray, God will answer.
> You'll call out for help and I'll say, 'Here I am.'
>
> If you get rid of unfair practices,
> quit blaming victims,
> quit gossiping about other people's sins.
> If you are generous with the hungry
> and start giving yourselves to the down-and-out,
> Your lives will begin to glow in the darkness,
> your shadowed lives will be bathed in sunlight.
> I will always show you where to go.
> I'll give you a full life in the emptiest of places –
> firm muscles, strong bones.
> You'll be like a well-watered garden,
> a gurgling spring that never runs dry.
> You'll use the old rubble of past lives to build anew,
> rebuild the foundations from out of your past.
> You'll be known as those who can fix anything,
> restore old ruins, rebuild and renovate,
> make the community livable again.

God promises He will answer their prayers again if they let love infiltrate and motivate all areas of their lives. The principle is the same as Jesus preached: that if we try to keep our lives we will lose them, but if we are willing to turn all areas of our lives over to Him and die to ourselves we will gain true life.

Throughout the Old Testament the prophets often deliver the same message: you're upholding the religious practices, but you're forgetting the heart of it so they have become empty rituals. For example Micah says:

> With what shall I come before the Lord
> and bow down before the exalted God?
> Shall I come before him with burnt offerings,
> with calves a year old?
> Will the Lord be pleased with thousands of rams,
> with ten thousand rivers of oil?
> Shall I offer my firstborn for my transgression,
> the fruit of my body for the sin of my soul?
> He has showed you, O man, what is good.
> And what does the Lord require of you?
> To act justly and to love mercy
> and to walk humbly with your God.
> (Micah 6:6–8)

The prophet clearly makes his point. Is God only pleased with huge, extravagant sacrifices like a thousand rivers of oil? Is the only way to please Him by sacrificing the most precious thing we have beside Him, our own children? No. God has made Himself clear: we are to 'act justly and to love mercy and to walk humbly' with Him. Over the next few chapters we will look at what it might mean for us to act justly and love mercy, because it is clear that this is something we cannot afford to miss.

What do we mean when we talk about the poor and injustice?

It's easy to see 'the poor' as a term for those who don't have enough money, but we also need to include in this definition those who suffer physically, mentally, spiritually, emotionally and socially. Often many of these elements are combined and are catalysts for each other. We can't say that poverty is something that only affects the developing world, as people on our very doorsteps, no matter where we live, may be poor in one form or another. We're talking not only about those who live below the financial poverty line but also about those who have been abused (physically, mentally and emotionally), those who have lost their homes and possessions through wars and natural disasters, those who are lonely or being bullied, those suffering from illness or addiction. . . The list goes on.

These situations are all unjust in the sense that they are not how things would be if God's kingdom ruled, but there is also another sense of injustice in the world: 'Injustice occurs when power is misused to take from others what God has given them, namely their life, dignity, liberty or the fruits of their love or labour' (Haugen). Examples of some of the ongoing injustices in our world today are abusive child labour, forced prostitution, corrupt police and governing bodies, child pornography, racial violence, terrorism and imprisonment without fair trial. The list seems endless.

The Bible makes it clear that doing something about this injustice is part of our worship to God: 'He who oppresses the poor shows contempt for their Maker, but whoever is kind to the needy honours God' (Proverbs 14:31). If we do not take justice seriously we are not taking God and His ways seriously. If we want to truly honour God we must stop seeing worship as something we do in church and take it out into society.

Giving and generosity

If we want to reflect God's heart and nature we also have to know that He is a generous God and act accordingly.

We're not very good at talking about money, even though we know that there are plenty of other areas of life we handle better when we're accountable to someone about them. As Christians we're happy to ask our friends how their relationship with God is, we have people who will regularly check in with us about how we're doing with our Bible reading and our prayer times, and we'd be comfortable challenging someone we loved who wasn't attending church. But when it comes to money we get shy and embarrassed and 'don't want to pry'. Even in the most honest of accountable relationships we rarely challenge each other or even dare to ask where our money goes. Maybe it's because the saying is true that the last part of us to be converted is usually our wallets.

When we talk about the poor, often our first reaction is to think, 'Well, I'm not exactly rich.' We look at celebrities who spend millions on numerous mansions around the globe, have their own private jets to fly them wherever they like, are never seen in the same item of clothing twice and think nothing of buying jewellery for the price of a small country, and we think, 'I can barely afford a new pair of trainers. I'm skint!' We don't consider ourselves rich simply because we can keep our food in a refrigerator, have a cupboard to put our clothes in, a roof over our heads and a bed to sleep in at night. These are things we consider basics and yet 75 per cent of the world's population do not have these luxuries, meaning if you have all of those things you are in the top 25 per cent of wealthy people in the entire world. If you shrunk the world proportionally into 100 people, only eight of them would have a computer and four would have an internet connection. The internet is again something we can easily take for granted, but those of us who are lucky enough to have access to it are in the top 4 per cent of the world's richest people. It is humbling to see on a world scale how rich we truly are. (The statistics are from www.miniatureearth.com.)

The way we spend our money is often a direct reflection of what's in our hearts: 'For where your treasure is, there your heart will be also' (Matthew 6:21). If someone who didn't know you picked up your bank statement, what would it tell them about you? Would it be clear what you're passionate about? Could they tell how much you love shopping for clothes or the latest gadgets, going for meals with family and friends, following a favourite sporting team or musician? None of these things are in and of themselves bad things to spend money on, but they may highlight our priorities.

People often say things like, 'All our money belongs to God,' which is true, but it doesn't provide a practical guide for knowing how to handle it. God has entrusted us with money with the aim of furthering His kingdom and we will have to give account for how we've used that money. Can you imagine sitting down with God and the world's largest calculator and going through all the money that has passed through your possession over the entire period of your life and explaining to God how it was used to serve Him?

Again King David is a great role model for us when it comes to giving: 'But who am I, and who are my people, that we should be able to give as generously as this? Everything comes from you, and we have given you only what comes from your hand' (1 Chronicles 29:14). He realises it all comes from God and it's a privilege to be able to give generously to God's work.

Traditionally in churches we pass round a plate when it comes to taking up the collection and we sing a hymn along with it. We changed this in our church after I saw the way the people in a poor township church in South Africa gave their money. They had so little and yet their giving was like an explosion of joy. They came out of their seats, singing and dancing and praising God with all their might as they brought their gifts to the baskets at the front. There was nothing passive or apathetic about their giving. They were so happy to be able to do it and were some of the most generous people I have ever come across, despite their poverty.

We read in 2 Corinthians 9:6–7: 'Whoever sows sparingly will also reap sparingly, and whoever sows generously will also reap generously. Each man should give what he has decided in his heart to give, not reluctantly or under compulsion, for God loves a cheerful giver.' The Greek word for 'cheerful' can alternatively be translated 'hilarious'; God is looking for generous people who take joy in giving and are extravagant with Him.

Tithing

Tithing is a very important part of our giving, but it shouldn't be where it stops. It's not a case of giving Him the first 10 per cent and then we get to keep the rest for ourselves. It is all a gift from God that we should offer back to Him in thanksgiving for His provision: 'You will be made rich in every way so that you can be generous on every occasion, and . . . your generosity will result in thanksgiving to God' (2 Corinthians 9:11). God gives to us so that we can bless others. He is generous to us so that we can be generous towards those around us. Again God's desire is not that we follow the letter of the law but the heart of it. As Jesus said, 'Woe to you, teachers of the law and Pharisees, you hypocrites! You give a tenth of your spices – mint, dill and cummin. But you have neglected the more important matters of the law – justice, mercy and faithfulness. You should have practised the latter, without neglecting the former' (Matthew 23:23).

Jesus was pointing out how hypocritical it was for the Pharisees to tithe on even their tiniest of garden herbs and yet not look after the poor. They were following their religious duty, but they were not honouring God as their Provider and using all that He had given to be generous to those in need. God is always interested in what is going on in our hearts. Do we desire money and financial security over Him or are we able to be generous and live in His freedom?

Right after Jesus teaches us that we 'cannot serve both God and Money' (Matthew 6:24), He reminds us why we don't need to get hung up about finances:

> Therefore I tell you, do not worry about your life, what you will eat or drink; or about your body, what you will wear. Is not life more important than food, and the body more important than clothes? ... So do not worry . . . your heavenly Father knows that you need them. But seek first his kingdom and his righteousness, and all these things will be given to you as well. (Matthew 6:25, 31–33)

There is an amazing freedom in knowing that we are under God's protection and care. We need to live in a way that reflects the fact that we know we have a God who loves and cares for us, who, with all the resources in heaven and on earth at His disposal, is more than capable of meeting our every need. If we truly believe that, we won't worry about living generously with our time, our money and our possessions and following God's call wherever He may lead. We love others because we are so overwhelmed by His great love for us. We go to those who have nothing, knowing that as we pursue the kingdom of God He will take care of our needs.

8

Compassion for a Broken World

The world we live in

800 million people don't have enough to eat, although there is more than enough food for everyone in the world. (Christian Aid)

40 million people are currently living with AIDS/HIV virus and 2.5 million of these are children. In Africa 13.4 million children have been orphaned by HIV.

Every single day 30,000 children die as a result of extreme poverty – despite the fact we have the knowledge, the resources and the opportunity to end this. (Make Poverty History website)

The developing world now spends $13 on debt repayment for every $1 it receives in grants.

In Africa more than 2 million infants die each year without reaching their fifth birthday. (Christian Aid)

85 out of 100 people in the world don't have running water at home. (Christian Aid)

1.4 million children die each year from lack of access to safe drinking water and adequate sanitation.

In 2004 24 per cent of children in England and Wales were living in single-parent families.

In England and Wales the people most likely to die a violent death are babies under one year old. They are four times more likely to be killed than the average person.

Around 200,000 people in the UK attempt to commit suicide each year.

The state of the world can be overwhelming. We look at these statistics and they begin to blur; our minds don't know how to process this kind of information. But these statistics are not just numbers – they are people, God's creation. Each one of those babies that dies before reaching their fifth birthday was knit together in their mother's womb, fearfully and wonderfully made (Psalm 139:13–14). Each one of those men, women and children who goes to sleep hungry at night bears God's image. Jesus' promise that we could have 'life to the full' was for every one of the almost 6,000 adults who committed suicide last year in the UK because life seemed so painful and hopeless to them.

Cultivating hearts of compassion

The first and most important thing to understand about growing a more compassionate heart is that the key is to get close to God. As we know Him more, we begin to share His heart and become aware of His ways. In Matthew 22 Jesus is asked about the most important commandment and He says, '"Love the Lord your God with all your heart and with all your soul and with all your mind." This is the first and greatest commandment. And the second is like it: "Love your neighbour as yourself"' (vv. 37–39).

There are five important words I want to pull out here: 'the second is like it'. We usually separate these two commands – we know they are our top priorities, but we feel they are surely quite different instructions. Not according to Jesus. Loving our brother is a vital part of loving God. As the apostle John says, 'If anyone says, "I love God," yet hates his brother, he is a liar. For anyone who does not love his brother, whom he has seen, cannot love God, whom he has not seen . . . Whoever loves God must also love his brother' (1 John 4:20–21).

We must act compassionately having had a revelation of God's heart, otherwise we are doing just what anyone with a big heart and no knowledge of God can do. The closer and more intimate we get with God, the more we recognise our selfish and self-indulgent ways and begin to share His heart for others.

Sometimes we have to choose not to turn away from the pain in the world. With so many channels on the TV we're used to just flicking over to the next station when the viewing doesn't suit us. We come home after a hard day at work or college and think, 'I can't face seeing those poor starving children again,' or, 'The news just depresses me. I think I'll watch something else.' It is often a difficult and conscious choice to watch and hear about another senseless murder, a new part of the world reeling from a natural disaster, miscarriages of justice or the growth of diseases like HIV. It's far easier to switch over and watch something more palatable – perhaps a soap opera, where problems are resolved easily and then quickly forgotten – rather than seeing real issues. But if we want to expand our hearts, we need sometimes to turn back and watch prayerfully, to share the Father's pain about the state of the world, to listen and see what we can do and to think about our response.

Because the truth is, if we don't look properly we'll never

cultivate true hearts of compassion. If we want our hearts to be changed then we need to get involved. Often I think we're afraid to see things fully because we know that once we have, we can never plead ignorance to God; we'll have blown that excuse out of the water.

After the first time I saw the pictures of starving people in Ethiopia which became so widespread in the 1980s, I knew God could call me to account at the end of my days; that He could ask, 'How did your life change after you saw that? You felt the Holy Spirit tugging at your heart – did you squash Him or allow Him to open up your heart and lead you to action?'

The trouble is, even pictures on the TV have become almost meaningless. We've become so used to seeing pictures of starving people on our screens and then turning over to see images of celebrity lifestyles, that both are equally unreal to us. We need some spiritual heart surgery to awaken us again to the pain in the world, and often the best way to do this is to see it for ourselves. Statistics are hard to relate to – we need to see the people behind them to cultivate hearts of compassion.

John Stott suggested that one of the best ways to pray is to hold your Bible in one hand and a newspaper in the other. We have to see what's going on in the world and what the Bible says about it and about how we should respond.

The thing that stretched my heart more than anything and made me realise I couldn't turn away any longer was meeting the street children from South Africa that I told you about at the start of the book who lived in a cardboard box. Meeting them changed my heart in a way that reading about them or seeing pictures on the TV never could. Seeing a friend stand before you weak with hunger, who wouldn't buy them food? If someone you cared about needed a doctor you would do everything in your power to make sure they got the attention they needed. That's how we respond when we are motivated by compassion and love, and when people become real to us rather than just statistics.

There are thousands of children like my friends in South Africa all over the world. Children who have none of the things we take for granted: the love of a family who will take care of us, the security of a home, the expectation that if we are hurting or ill we will be able to get treatment, and the ability to wash so that we can feel clean and decent every day.

The God I know is broken-hearted over what we've allowed to happen to some of His children. Justice is to say, 'Your kingdom come, Your will be done on earth as it is in heaven.'

Of course you don't have to look past your own street to find people who are hurting and in need of love and support. One of my friends, Emily, moved with three others to a house in an average suburban town and decided they would see what they could do to bless the lives of their neighbours. Here is her story:

When we moved in we found there was a woman living next door with four children aged between four and eleven. Her husband (father to three of them) would come and go depending on whether he'd found another woman to be with, so there wasn't a lot of stability in the house. He was also a drug dealer and saw nothing wrong in showing the kids how to burgle from others and it was a regular thing for one of them to be in trouble with the police.

Domestic violence was commonplace in the household; the parents would shout at and hit the kids on a daily basis and throw things at each other during screaming rows. Unsurprisingly the kids were violent and aggressive themselves; this was just a normal way to express your feelings to them, but it got them into lots of trouble. The eldest was suspended from school for violent behaviour at the age of eleven and the youngest was almost expelled for a vicious attack on an older pupil – she was just five years old at the time.

Their mother struggled to help them with even the basics; she didn't know how to cook, so she would send the kids round to the chip shop each night to get their tea (when they saw fruit and vegetables at our house they couldn't tell us what they were). She was illiterate and so couldn't help them with their homework and hadn't even taught them how to brush their teeth or to wash their hands after going to the toilet.

One of the things we found hardest to see was the emotional abuse they suffered. They were constantly told they were useless, that there was no hope for them, that they would amount to nothing and would end up in prison. They even called one of them 'the child of the devil'.

Because of all of this the kids craved adult attention and affirmation. We knew that if we wanted to help we had to commit to being part of these children's lives. There was no point in giving them money or just taking them on the odd day out to get a break; we wanted to be a positive influence on the whole of their lives.

We invited them into our house and said they could come over whenever they wanted. We showed them how to cook and taught them about basic nutrition and what was good for them. We took them to the park, taught them about hygiene, helped with their homework (we even had to teach the eldest boy, who was by now 13, what the letters of the alphabet were and the months of the year). We took them to Sunday school and tried to affirm them, to find out what they were good at and encourage them to develop their gifts; we explained why school was a *positive thing and how it could open up opportunities for them in the future.*

We let them do jobs for us around the house to earn money and showed them how to do a basic invoice so they could start learning some job skills. We also tried really hard to get to know the parents, to invite them round for a drink and to build a relationship and a trust with them too. The mum used to come round if her husband had left her again or if she felt she needed a refuge from him when he was in a violent temper.

It was hard work and sometimes we would get fed up or just worn out. It was disheartening when they stole from us, but we'd try and keep reminding each other why we had chosen to get involved. We did see huge changes in them too; one of them still comes to church five years later, they softened and began to trust us (not an easy thing for them), they had better social skills and so began to make friends, they started regularly attending school and they managed to stay out of trouble with the police.

Who are we to change anything?

The trouble with looking at the state of the world is that it can overwhelm us. Things can look so bleak that we lose hope and feel small and helpless in the face of the atrocities we witness. It seems as though any effort we could make wouldn't make even the smallest dent, never mind much of an impact. For every family that we can get involved in like Emily and her friends, aren't there hundreds more that we can do nothing about? The absolute worst thing we can do is to let this feeling of helplessness paralyse us.

When a journalist asked U2's Bono about his work in Africa and why he thought he could make a difference he replied,

'. . . we can't lose because we're putting our shoulder to a door that God Almighty has already opened' (Bono on Bono). And that's the truth of it. This is God's idea first. This is God's agenda and I believe He will lead, guide and help us as we go.

I was encouraged and inspired to read in Good News about Injustice by Gary A. Haugen about a number of Christians who brought about huge changes for justice through their faithful walk with God. In the late 1800s Kate Bushnell, an evangelical Christian, was devastated to see many girls being forced into prostitution in Wisconsin. With the police turning a blind eye and the doctors encouraging these rapes due to the additional income of examining the injured girls, she was fighting a tough battle. Putting herself at great physical risk she undertook investigative work and presented her evidence until people were forced to take notice. Eventually a bill was passed in her name that put an end to this horrendous practice.

It seems almost impossible to imagine it now, but at the beginning of the last century enforced child labour was still a serious issue in North America. Edgar Murphy was a minister from Alabama who began writing about the horrors he had seen. He distributed copies of his reports throughout the USA (often funded from his own pocket) in order to raise awareness of what was happening. Murphy was a founding member of the committee whose work brought about the abolition of child slavery.

Both of these cases would have looked almost impossible battles to fight before Kate Bushnell and Edgar Murphy took up their cause. I'm sure there were many times they both doubted the effectiveness of what they were doing and whether they could really make a difference. No doubt there were great personal sacrifices along the way of money, time, safety and reputation, yet they stayed true to God's heart and in doing so changed the lives of many millions of people.

William Booth was the founder of the Salvation Army. A Methodist minister in the 1800s, he realised there was a large part of society that the church wasn't reaching. So he took his preaching from the pulpit to the poor and spent himself on telling them about the love of Jesus. From this humble start grew the organisation that today operates in over 100 countries around the world and serves millions of people each year. They run many initiatives to give practical help, from homeless shelters to hospitals, addiction centres to community youth programmes, counselling to education centres. What started as a desire in one man's heart to reach the lost became an international mission that is bearing fruit almost 100 years after his death and will no doubt continue to do so for many more years.

There are many stories we know that encourage us that one person's faith can impact the world. I'm sure there are countless more Christians whose stories have never been told, but their day-to-day living and their desire to follow God has made a radical difference and changed people's lives and futures. We're not in it for the glory, but we should take heart that each seed God sows in our hearts, if nurtured and acted on, can yield more fruit than we could possibly imagine.

God's promise of blessing

God doesn't promise us the fight for justice will be easy – there is a great cost involved – but He does promise us He will be with us and reward us. One verse I have always loved is Proverbs 19:17: 'He who is kind to the poor lends to the Lord. . .' What an idea! That we can give God a gift and that we can lend something to Him by being kind to those who have less than we do. The end of the sentence isn't bad either: '. . . and he will reward him for what he has done.' Again we see this truth that as we give to God, we see more of His generosity and blessings in our own lives.

And God doesn't make this promise just once. Take a look at these verses:

> A generous man will himself be blessed,
> for he shares his food with the poor.
> (Proverbs 22:9)

Give, and it will be given to you. A good measure, pressed down, shaken together and running over, will be poured into your lap. For with the measure you use, it will be measured to you. (Luke 6:38)

It is clear that this is God's way, as we have already discussed. He is a generous God and He wants our lives to reflect His generosity. We have to be careful, however, that we don't make assumptions about what God's blessing will look like. Sometimes we look at it like the ultimate fail-safe 'get rich quick' scheme: we give away and God gives us back more. Bingo! But we know it doesn't really work like that because God knows that earthly riches are not the highest reward He can give. Yes, He often does bless us with money and financial provision, wonderful homes and promotions at work, but as we give our hearts, our time, our money and our possessions, we may find the blessing we receive is a closer understanding of God's presence in our daily walk. It may be that we notice a change in our hearts and attitudes, an increased peace and lack of worry over His provision, as we know we are in safe hands. He might want to bless us with a heart that aches for a broken world, being humble enough to count serving God in any capacity and at any cost a privilege, being abandoned to the idea that possessions count for little and pleasing God counts for a lot.

> Good will come to him who is generous and lends freely,
> who conducts his affairs with justice.
> (Psalm 112:5)

9

What Can I Do?

So we've talked about *what* justice is and how close to God's heart it is, and *why* we should take action in terms of our worship of God impacting all areas of our lives. The next question for us when considering active compassion is *how*? This chapter is devoted to the practical steps we can all take to make the fight for justice part of our everyday lives.

And that's the key – it doesn't have to be about making a decision to sell all we have and then giving the money to the poor, but it needs to be about building it into our lives in steps that we can manage, constantly bringing this as an area before God and asking Him what else we can be doing. Some people might be able to make radical changes and stick with them, but if you're anything like me, you'll get all excited, promise you'll change all your ways, fail within hours and then, disheartened, decide to give up. Like most areas of our lives, we start with small steps and then keep growing and developing until we can walk, jog, run and eventually go the long distance. I would really encourage you, as you read through this chapter, to think about the steps you can take. There may be loads you are already doing, which is great, but keep going for it and keep your eyes and heart open for more.

Of course, this is not an exhaustive list – there are endless numbers of creative ways you can be fighting for justice. These are just some ideas to get you thinking.

Pray

The first thing we can all be doing, and should be making a regular practice, is to pray about the injustices in the world. We all have testimony from our own lives of ways we have cried out to God and seen His mighty hand at work. God makes us many promises regarding prayer; for example, '. . . will not God bring about justice for his chosen ones, who cry out to him day and night?' (Luke 18:7) and, 'If my people, who are called by my name, will humble themselves and pray and seek my face and turn from their wicked ways, then will I hear from heaven and will forgive their sin and will heal their land' (2 Chronicles 7:14).

We may need to start praying by asking God to give us His compassion. If you don't feel it, don't try and fake it, but be honest and say, 'God, I know I should care more about this than I do at the moment. Please mould my heart to long for the things You long for. Give me a desire to pray and serve and seek Your kingdom in my life.'

Prayer is so much more than putting requests before God; it's about building relationship with Him and when we talk to Him and listen we begin to share His heart. As Richard Foster has said, 'Prayer is the central avenue God uses to change us.' I don't know about you, but I know that my heart needs some changing if it is to better reflect my Father's heart for this world.

We can't tackle these issues in our own strength or simply out of a sense of duty, as it's not sustainable long term and we'll be in danger of getting worn out, burnt out and resentful. We need to be motivated from a place of love, starting with a love for our God and, as we begin to share His heart, a love for the people He wants to send us to.

Often during times of intercession when people begin to discover God's heart in this way, they find themselves unable to speak and they simply weep as they share something of His pain and anguish over a broken world. They find that words just don't seem to be enough, and they are helpless to express what they feel in their hearts, so they intercede with tears. Paul wrote to the Romans: 'the Spirit helps us in our weakness. We do not know what we ought to pray for, but the Spirit himself intercedes for us with groans that words cannot express' (Romans 8:26).

Where to start

Many Christian charities produce free prayer guides, which can be a great place to start. They're ideal for giving you a focus, especially if there's a particular charity whose work you're interested in. They'll often send you newsletters too that will keep you updated on what they're doing and the good things they've seen God do.

Watching the daily news can be a heart-breaking experience, but it is also an amazing aid to prayer. Looking through the paper or turning on the radio or TV and watching with God's eyes prompts us to ask Him to be involved in these situations, to bring about His justice, to raise up more people to tackle the issues that are rife in our world. Sometimes we feel we can do little more than pray for the family mourning the loss of a child who has been senselessly murdered, but there may also be times and situations when God calls us to be the very answers to the prayers we pray, because so often prayer leads to action.

Pete Greig began the powerful 24–7 prayer movement that started people around the world opening prayer rooms so that for days, weeks and months at a time there were people praying round the clock. Pete was told by Brennan Manning, author of *The Ragamuffin Gospel*: 'The most powerful thing that can happen in the place of prayer is that you become the prayer. You leave the room as Jesus' hands and feet on earth' (*Red Moon Rising*, p. 95).

We've been realising that there is a place for weeping over the pain and suffering in the world, and that God answers prayer sometimes in the most spectacular of ways, but the truth is that the tears themselves don't feed anyone. Yes, we should cry out. Yes, we should bring this pain before God. But sometimes we have to get up and get out and be the answer to the very prayers we've prayed. We can't shout from the comfort of our churches and living rooms 'We love you' to people who need food, because the words are hollow to their ears unless they see we are willing to share our food with them: 'Suppose a brother or sister is without clothes and daily food. If one of you says to him, 'Go, I wish you well; keep warm and well fed,' but does nothing about his physical needs, what good is it?' (James 2:15–16).

Give financially

We've already talked about how important it is that we use our money to bless others, whether as part of our tithe or in addition to it. We should all be looking to be generous with the money God has given us and put it to good use. There are so many charities that would use even £2 a month to make a difference to people's lives. There's no right or wrong way to pick a charity – we all have different causes that we can relate to or things that we are passionate about – so see what is in your heart and where you would like to give.

Child sponsorship

One great way to give which has tangible results is to sponsor a child. For about £15 a month you can literally change someone's life. Sometimes it's the difference between life and death. Your money provides the essentials of clean water, food, basic healthcare and immunisation against disease. Often, in addition, it provides education and life-skills training courses that give people a means to generate their own income and change their future. If you're not currently earning, or not earning very much, you could make a commitment with a group of friends or your cell group and see how far your collective money will go.

Giving charitable gifts

It is estimated that every year £355 billion is spent on Christmas presents in Europe alone. I think it's a wonderful thing that we can express our love and appreciation for people by buying gifts, but sometimes it feels as though things get a bit out of control. We have far more than we could possibly ever need and yet we spend so much on getting even more. A number of charities have thought of a way that we could use birthdays and Christmas as another opportunity to bless others in need and be more outward looking in our approach to buying presents. They've launched alternative gift catalogues from which you can buy presents that could transform a life, a family or even a whole community. With prices ranging from a few pounds to a few hundred pounds, offering everything from a fruit tree that provides income and food for a family living in poverty year after year for less than the price of a CD to a water system that will save members of a village from having to travel miles each and every day just to get water that isn't contaminated.

Fund-raising

Most of us don't have an endless supply of cash and find it frustrating when we hear of all the worthy causes that could do with more money and we can't give it. Creative fund-raising could be the answer, with anything from local car washes, a sponsored run/fast/silence/weight-loss, holding a jumble sale, fund-raising dinners and parties, raffles or auction. . . The possibilities are endless. Get your church home group or youth group involved and enjoy the fun, knowing you're doing something that will change people's lives.

Through being generous with our money we can make a huge difference to the lives of people who have very little, but God doesn't want us to seek justice only in our finances.

Shop wisely – buy fair trade

Have you ever stopped to think about your power as a consumer? Most of the time we only see ourselves as individuals so don't imagine we can make much difference, but when it's combined our buying power has a very loud voice. Companies spend millions upon millions of pounds trying to get us to buy their products. If we start 'voting with our feet' and taking our custom to places that have good ethical policies, then people will sit up and begin to take notice.

Be an ethical consumer

Nestlé is one of the world's largest companies and in the late 1970s it was found to be exploiting new mothers in developing countries, and the Infant Formula Action Coalition called for a boycott. Nestlé was offering new mothers powder from which to make a milk drink for their babies, and by the time the 'free gift' had finished the mother's own milk had dried up. This left them with only one alternative: to continue to buy the expensive powder and mix it with unclean water. This was causing many infant deaths and malnutrition. It seemed strange at first to think that you'd make much of a difference if you stopped buying their most famous brand of coffee and substituted a Cadbury's chocolate bar for a Nestlé one. But when thousands started to do it and their sales plummeted, they began to take notice and during the 1980s changed their policies for the better. Nestlé says it no longer uses such aggressive and unethical marketing policies, but organisations like International Baby Food Action Network and Baby Milk Action (www.babymilkaction.org) say the company still violates agreed codes of conduct and should be boycotted (www.corporatewatch.org.uk 20th January 2006).

Many companies use child labour, pay unfair wages or force workers to toil in unreasonable conditions in order to keep their costs down and make cheap products. If we want to be ethical consumers we should be looking at companies' policies to see whether they pay the producers a fair rate or whether they use slave labour. It's really tempting to think, 'But this T-shirt's so cheap!' but don't forget that somebody somewhere always has to pay the price. However, while boycotting worked well with Nestlé and its unethical practices, where there are issues of slave labour, boycotting may do more harm than good to the individuals concerned. If people stop buying the products this can cause factories to close and put people out of work. Even earning a small amount is clearly more desirable than earning nothing at all, so it is more effective for us to be making our voice heard by asking to see companies' policies and making our interest known in fair-trade products.

Lobby

> Speak up for those who cannot speak for themselves,
> for the rights of all who are destitute.
> Speak up and judge fairly;
> defend the rights of the poor and needy.
> (*Proverbs 31:8–9*)

In this era of mass communication and easy internet access, lobbying has never been easier. Filling in postcards, writing letters and forwarding emails all add your voice to the growing number of people who are asking for governments and companies to take responsibility for bringing about justice. Charities are keen for people's support and will usually provide details of petitions you can sign, send you free postcards to use, provide you with draft letters and give you all the tools you need to speak up for those who cannot speak up for themselves.

As Martin Luther King said, 'We will have to repent in this generation not merely for the cruel words and actions of the bad people, but for the appalling silence of the good people.'

Bank wisely

Did you know that the money in your bank account could be invested in the arms trade, pornography, organisations that do not uphold basic human rights and exploit their workers, and companies that test their products on animals and damage the environment? Ask your bank about how ethical their investment policies are and if you're not happy with the answers move your money somewhere it won't be used for harm.

Consider short-term mission

In a few months' time our church, Soul Survivor Watford, is going to Durban, South Africa, for a house party, and I can't tell you how excited I am that we're going as a family. We've often held house parties where God has met with us and blessed us, and I know this will be a house party with a difference as we look to be a blessing to that community. We're planning on having time together to meet with God and time to relax, but we intend to spend our afternoons working with the street kids, in the poorest shanty town communities and at an orphanage for children whose parents have died from AIDS.

This is such an amazing opportunity for us to share in an adventure together, particularly for those of us who haven't been exposed to the kind of poverty we will encounter there. We want to be a practical blessing and have our eyes and our hearts opened to some of the suffering in our world.

There are many ways you can get involved in short-term missions, whether it's through reputable agencies or joining members of your church who need help with their missionary work. If you work with people who know the area and the problems, you can make sure your presence is a blessing and your efforts are directed in the best possible way.

You may want to take a gap year before, after or during studies or work; or you may be able to give a few weeks. If you can make the time there are certainly enough places where it could be put to good use.

Commit to long-term mission

There are many whose heart's desire is to be a missionary in the traditional sense of living overseas in a deprived area and working full time with those who are most in need. Friends of mine from Holland, Daniel and Marlies, have left the comforts of home for Kitale in northern Kenya to serve God among the people there.They told me:

Since we were children we've both always had an interest in Africa and loved the idea of living there, but at the age of 24 we were settled in Holland, had been married for four years and were working for a Christian organisation. We were happy there and still felt there was plenty for us to do with the young people we were working with, but after a trip to the poor region of northern Kenya we began to feel God was calling us to move there.

We felt so under-prepared – we'd never been to Bible college and we didn't consider ourselves to have any special skills we could offer. We were just two people who wanted to serve God wherever He called us to. Our passion was the same in Kenya as it was in Holland: to see young people meet with God and make a difference in their society.

In the 18 months we've been here so much has already happened. We've opened an orphanage which has given a home to six kids and we have a food programme for almost 100 primary school children that ensures they get at least one warm meal a day. With help from churches and organisations abroad we've furnished a primary school, built a centre for the church and community to use, given out clothes and food to local villages, and are currently looking into starting a first-aid programme. It sounds like a lot, but there's so much still to do. We're building a centre for the young people to meet and pray, and are trying to raise funds for a home for teenage mothers and their babies. Of course these aren't things we could have ever done single-handedly; we've had a lot of support, both financial and practical, from local people and organisations.

One of the amazing things about long-term missionary work is that you really get to know the people and the culture so much more than if you just visit for a short time. We're really enjoying building relationships and growing to love people we would never have otherwise met. Of course we've missed our friends and family. God has given us grace for that, but to be honest it's still been hard at times, particularly now that we are expecting our first child, a time when you really value being close to those you love. But we are committed to being here for as long as God calls us.

We're totally dependent on God from a financial point of view, both to clothe and feed ourselves and for the work we want to do in Kenya, but He has been very faithful to us even when the situation has seemed hopeless. It's a truth we all know that God is able to do miracles if we put ourselves in the position where we need them!

We would definitely encourage anyone who's thinking about mission work of this kind to forget the nerves and just go for it! It's easy to look at ourselves and see our weaknesses, so we find *it helps to remember that many of the people in the Bible thought they weren't up to the task, but God used them regardless. We've found that the most important skills to develop are to be humble and to come ready to serve and to learn. Make sure you have a strong group of friends who will pray for you and with you and can give you good advice. Although it's not always easy, it is so exciting to step out and take a risk on God, to try things that we know will fail unless He turns up. If you're thinking of doing it, then keep asking God to open doors and show you where to go, what to do and how to do it.*

If you think God may be calling you to this kind of missionary work then chat and pray it through with trusted friends and leaders. Prepare yourself as much as possible by researching the place you are going to and talking to others who have walked a similar path.

Bless your local town

Of course, you don't have to go abroad to get involved. For most of us there are plenty of people in our home town who need help and support in some area of their lives.

A few years ago a member of our church, Taryn, had a vision for setting up a pregnancy crisis centre. She was passionate about supporting young girls who found themselves in the frightening position of being pregnant when they hadn't planned to be. Taryn was desperate that these women should have somewhere to go and someone to turn to who would love and support them and provide a listening ear. Many others in the church caught the vision and the centre now runs not only a pregnancy crisis counselling service, but also a mums and tots group for the teenage girls and a drop-in centre where they can get support, access the internet to apply for jobs and benefits, receive clothes and goods for their babies and hang out and form relationships with others in a similar position.

An organisation I've always admired is XLP, a charity that works in its local area (the south east boroughs of London) aiming to meet the social, educational and behavioural needs of young people. This involves everything from running school assemblies, homework and lunchtime/after-school clubs, to literacy support and music and dance lessons. XLP works hard to show God's love to young people in a culturally relevant way, through building relationships and working with community groups, local authorities, local police and churches to provide the practical help needed in an area. Many of the young people it helps have achieved little at school, have few ambitions and are known as troublemakers. What they desperately need is someone to give them a helping hand, invest in them rather than writing them off and help them improve their lives; exactly what the XLP aims to do.

Every town, city and village is different, so see what the need is in your area and match it up with things you're passionate about and able to do. There may be a volunteer bureau that will give you some ideas and put you in touch with various groups that need an extra pair of hands. You could visit people in hospitals and prisons, the elderly who may not get to see another smiling face all week or offer to help out with a trust for homeless people. There are currently more needs than people to meet them, so whatever your gifts there's sure to be a way you can use them to bless others in your community.

Someone once told me that if you want to know the theology of any church, you should look at its architecture. If in the centre there is a big pulpit decorated with a huge golden eagle, you can easily conclude that teaching is key to that church, or if the altar table seems the most visible thing, it may be a Catholic church, where communion is key. In other places, like our church, we have wires and amps all over the place, so it's easy to tell we place a priority on sung worship. If you have visited Soul Survivor Watford over the last few years you will have noticed pretty quickly that we have a large black bin placed in front of the stage. You might think that this is an odd and unsightly choice, but we use it as part of our worship. As we sing a song and come forward to put money in the offering baskets, we also encourage people to bring items of food and other useful goods and put them in the bin. These are later distributed by our local social services team. This is such a simple way to bless our community. When you're doing the weekly shop it's easy to put in a few extra tins or some nappies and know that these will bless a local family who are struggling to put food on the table. The big black bin may look ugly, but it's a practical reminder to us of the poor and helps us to remember that our worship doesn't stop with singing.

There are so many things we can do and there's so much need everywhere we look. We all have different hearts, different amounts of time, different resources and talents. The point is that we're all called to do something. I know I want to build things into my life that I can do on an ongoing basis so that my heart is continually being stretched and changed. As I've written this chapter and thought again about some of the different ways we can get involved, I've felt challenged to make the fight for justice a part of my daily walk, as vital as prayer and praise as an expression of my relationship with God.

Why not stop for a few moments and think about what you have just read? Are there any areas that particularly excited you? There may be some things you are already doing, like giving regularly to charity, and some that can be built into your daily life quite easily and quickly, like praying. There may be other things that you need to spend some time thinking and praying about; to consider making a reality. Talk to your friends and family. See what you can do together and find people who share your desire to serve God in this way and keep one another accountable and encouraged on the journey. Let's not leave this to other people like the celebrities who are currently flying the flag for justice. This is something that we are all capable of getting involved in. We can make a real difference to this world, no matter how small our steps seem.

> And God is able to make all grace abound to you, so that in all things at all times, having all that you need, you will abound in every good work. (2 Corinthians 9:8)

Further information

Child sponsorship

Visit www.compassion.com or www.actionaid.org.uk or www.worldvision.org.uk

Charitable gifts

Try www.greatgifts.org or www.oxfamunwrapped.com

Fair trade

See the campaigning section of www.tearfund.org for more details on Fair Trade products or visit www.maketradefair.com for more information.

Being an ethical consumer

Visit youth.tearfund.org and see their 'Lift the Label' campaign (you can download a copy of their *Ethical Directory*) or buy the *Lift the Label* book by David Westlake and Esther Stansfield. This includes information about investing your money wisely.

Mission work

A good place to start for short-term mission is www.christian vocations.org which has advice, vacancies and resources, including a short-term service directory that you can order.

Tearfund have long- and short-term mission vacancies advertised on their website for both the UK and overseas (www.tearfund.org/jobseekers).

Part 4
CONCLUSION

10

How Do They All Work Together?

Love and action

. . .the greatest of these is love. (1 Corinthians 13:13)

I have to confess that when I became a youth worker at St Andrew's Chorleywood there were times when I thought I was quite important. Before, during and after services I could be seen rushing around feeling very busy and significant. One day, when I was in the midst of my work, an old lady from the congregation called to me as I went past, 'Mike, won't you come and sit down for a minute?'

I sighed heavily and looked at my watch, hoping to convey with that and a raised eyebrow how very precious my time was and that she was keeping me from my work.

'Come on, Mike,' she encouraged. So I dutifully sat, willing her to be quick. 'Don't you just love Jesus, Mike?' she asked quietly, a look of such pleasure on her face. 'Doesn't it make you so happy to know Him and to know He loves you?'

I'm sure I looked surprised; I'd been expecting a half-hour lecture on varicose veins.

'Anytime you're passing by, pop in and see me; the door's always open and I'd love to pray and worship Jesus with you.'

I was truly humbled. There I was, thinking I was so busy and important serving Jesus, and what Hilda wanted to do was talk about how much she loved Him. She had chosen what was better; not to rush around hoping to impress God and others with acts of service, but to love God with all her heart and to let that love overflow in her life. The truth was that there was a smell about Hilda, and no, it wasn't that she'd forgotten to wash. Paul said, 'For we are to God the aroma of Christ among those who are being saved and those who are perishing' (2 Corinthians 2:15), and Hilda stank strongly. Not like I did, of hard work and self-importance, but of the fragrance of Christ.

Whenever I'm tempted to put serving God before my relationship with Him, I remember Hilda and her wonderful friendship with her heavenly Father. I remember that it's easy to get caught up in the busyness – after all, haven't we just been looking at the great needs around us and some of the things we can do to try and address them? But we have to remember that the very first and therefore the greatest commandment is to 'Love the Lord your God with all your heart and with all your soul and with all your mind and with all your strength' (Mark 12:30). Jesus didn't say, 'Serve the Lord your God with all your heart.' He used the word 'love'. We often get busy with the serving bit and then love God from the worn-out dregs of what's left over.

Richard Foster says in Celebration of Discipline: 'Service flows out of worship. Service instead of worship is idolatry.' It's easy to fill our time and not make space to meet with God, but we mustn't replace our relationship with God with doing things in His name. As Foster points out, this is sin. Even Jesus, in all He did while on earth, regularly made hanging out with His Father a priority. If Jesus could afford to take time out from what He was doing to spend it with His Father, it would be extreme arrogance to think that we're doing anything so important that we can't do the same.

We see God's heart on this in Revelation 2, where He commends the church in Ephesus for persevering and enduring hardships in His name, but there's something not quite right: 'Yet I hold this against you: You have forsaken your first love' (v. 4). The most important thing for us to remember is that we must put our love for God first. As Paul said, 'If I give all I possess to the poor and surrender my body to the flames, but have not love, I gain nothing' (1 Corinthians 13:3).

The familiar story of Mary again highlights that worship is our first priority. When Jesus was having dinner with friends, Mary poured over His feet expensive perfume worth about the equivalent of a year's wages. Although Judas had ulterior motives (to steal the money for himself), he asked a valid question: wouldn't it have been better to have sold the perfume and given the money to the poor rather than 'wasting' it on Jesus? Given what we've seen of God's heart for the poor, wouldn't Jesus agree with Judas? Not at all. He said, 'You will always have the poor among you, but you will not always have me' (John 12:8).

Actions demonstrate genuine love

Love is the most important thing, but the truth is, it's pretty much impossible to love God and not love others. St Augustine said, 'Love God and do what you like.' He knew that to love God means to grow to become like Him and to share His heart, so 'what we like' starts to fall in line with what God wants. When we put the worship first, the other things should fall into place.

James addresses this issue of our actions going hand in hand with our faith and relationship with God:

> Dear friends, do you think you'll get anywhere in this if you learn all the right words but never do anything? Does merely talking about faith indicate that a person really has it? For instance, you come upon an old friend dressed in rags and half-starved and say, 'Good morning, friend! Be clothed in Christ! Be filled with the Holy Spirit!' and walk off without providing so much as a coat or a cup of soup – where does that get you? Isn't it obvious that God-talk without God-acts is outrageous nonsense? I can already hear one of you agreeing by saying, 'Sounds good. You take care of the faith department, I'll handle the works department.' Not so fast. You can no more show me your works apart from your faith than I can show you my faith apart from my works. Faith and works, works and faith, fit together hand in glove. (James 2:14–18, *The Message*)

He goes so far as to say that if you try and divide your faith and your works, you 'end up with a corpse on your hands' because 'faith expresses itself in works'. Acts of kindness towards other people, whether that be helping a friend or sending money to someone overseas you've never met before, are first and foremost acts of love and devotion to God.

In the Gospel of Matthew we read the story Jesus tells of the day of judgement. He says that all the nations will be before Him and He will separate them into two categories: the sheep and the goats. To the sheep on His right-hand side He will say:

> 'Come, you who are blessed by my Father; take your inheritance, the kingdom prepared for you since the creation of the world. For I was hungry and you gave me something to eat, I was thirsty and you gave me something to drink, I was a stranger and you invited me in, I needed clothes and you clothed me, I was sick and you looked after me, I was in prison and you came to visit me.' Then the

righteous will answer him, 'Lord, when did we see you hungry and feed you, or thirsty and give you something to drink? When did we see you a stranger and invite you in, or needing clothes and clothe you? When did we see you sick or in prison and go to visit you?' The King will reply, 'I tell you the truth, whatever you did for one of the least of these brothers of mine, you did for me.' (Matthew 25:34–40)

The sheep didn't even recognise what they were doing. They looked after the stranger and the hungry without realising that God saw each and every act and accepted it as love and devotion for Himself.

The goats on His right-hand side, however, hear a very different story. They are told they did not love God by looking after the homeless and the prisoner, so they must depart from God's presence for eternity.

Every act of kindness for someone in need is first and foremost an act of love for Jesus. It's not about being able to say that we've done our quota of good deeds or trying to hook people in. We are called to love because God loves; we are called to give because God gives; we are called to be merciful because God is merciful.

We're not trying to earn God's love, approval or favour through our works: 'For it is by grace you have been saved, through faith – and this not from yourselves, it is the gift of God – not by works, so that no-one can boast' (Ephesians 2:8–9). The deeds don't save us or make us right with God, but they are an outward sign that we know we are saved and have received God's love, because when we have, we can't help but love others.

What happens when you separate worship, evangelism and justice?

Worship without justice

We've seen that worship is to be the top priority, but what happens if we do this but don't seek justice for the poor? We see God's view of this in Amos 5 when He rebukes His people:

I hate, I despise your religious feasts;
I cannot stand your assemblies.
Even though you bring me burnt offerings and grain offerings,
I will not accept them.
Though you bring choice fellowship offerings,
I will have no regard for them.
Away with the noise of your songs!
I will not listen to the music of your harps.
But let justice roll on like a river,
righteousness like a never-failing stream!
(Amos 5:21–24)

Of course, God wasn't objecting to the feasts and the offerings in and of themselves; it was the heart behind them. These people were living it up at the expense of the poor. While they were religiously offering their tithes and sacrifices, they were corrupt and dishonest in their business practices, court judges were being bribed and they were oppressing the poor. God will not stand for hypocrisy, and what He makes clear here is that if our actions do not back up our words, then the words mean nothing. God doesn't hide from us what He wants us to do; it's not a guessing game that we may or may not get right. He spells it out again: I want justice, I want your actions to back up your words.

Spiritual and secular

Our culture often separates the spiritual from the secular and so we lead what would be called a dualistic lifestyle. The Hebrews understood that we are made up of body, mind and spirit, and they saw all these elements working together as one. For example, we've seen worship as something we do on a Sunday at church, whereas it should be expressed in each area of our life and society.

So much of what we do in church is inaccessible to those who are unchurched. It doesn't mean anything to them, so it's not easy for them to come and be a part of it. We have to look at all areas of our lives and see how we can build bridges with those who are outside of the church. Over the last few years it has been troubling me that most of the creativity in music, art and drama in today's culture comes from outside of the church. This can't be right, as those of us in relationship with God have the Creator's spirit inside of us. The Holy Spirit is the spirit of creativity, but so often it seems as though we're not willing to take risks in creativity because we're afraid of making mistakes. We need to be released and to release others to go on an adventure.

If we play it safe we'll sit in our pews doing what we've always done, and we'll pass on the same cautiousness to generation after generation. It's a big challenge to make our music contemporary and culturally relevant. In my opinion the best worship music would be a Christian version of Simon and Garfunkel or, if we really wanted to be cutting edge, Meatloaf. Sadly this generation don't share my tastes in music – a tragedy in my opinion, but I'm trying to deal with it.

I've come across lots of young Christian musicians who feel

trapped and constricted. They have two passions, worship and evangelism, and they have been made to feel as though they have to choose which route to take. I think it is desperately important for the growth of the church that we release people to realise it doesn't have to be a choice and that both can and should work together. Many have been bound by the fear that they are being 'worldly' in their desire to take their music outside of the church, when this is in fact what God has called them to do. We need to ask God to forgive us for the times when our attitudes and fears have held people back, even if our intentions have been good, where we have misunderstood God's call on their lives.

There are obvious examples of Christians who have spearheaded the way, from Kevin Prosch to Delirious? and One hundredhours. They've all had different approaches and forced us to question what worship is, what performance is and how you use them both to glorify God's name.

And it would be ridiculous to think we need to take only creativity in music out from the church and into the world. This should be about all areas and all gifts. Whether we have a talent for sculpture, creating websites, creative writing or acting, we need to see it as an expression of worship and we need to invite the Holy Spirit to come into that, to bless our gifts and increase them and to use them for His name.

We've seen it throughout history with poets such as Gerard Manley Hopkins and Christina Rossetti, who proclaimed Christ through their writings, from classic novels like *Pilgrim's Progress* to the Chronicles of Narnia, which are being born again in a series of films for this generation. We must use our creativity and all of our gifts to declare God's name and nature, as this is both part of our worship and part of our evangelism.

Where does the church fit in?

Until the reign of Queen Anne about 200 years ago, the church was at the heart of the nation and it saw no divide between sacred and secular work. It was the main provider of education, as most schools were run by the Church of England, and it ran the health service, with many Christians involved in running hospitals. The church also provided social services and looked after those who were starving and in need. If someone found themselves in trouble, they would often go to the church.

This meant that the church was at the heart of the spiritual, social and political life of the country. Gradually it then retreated into a spiritual gospel, meaning its main focus was to say to people, 'Come and believe, repent and you'll go to heaven.' Christians withdrew and the state began to take over the roles of education, healthcare and social services. As the church became detached from these needs, fewer people wanted to hear its spiritual message. Now, in our day, people often complain that the church is not rooted in real life or living in the real world. We're beginning to discover again that we need a voice in society with a biblical agenda.

Often the church has attached itself to particular party agendas, so when we speak up for unborn babies' rights we are following a traditionally right-wing agenda and when we campaign for countries suffering from debts imposed on them by Western nations we take on a left-wing agenda. But it has to be about more than falling on this side or that. We must stand up for ecology as well as personal freedom; we want to free people from living under dictatorship as well as make sure that we do not rape the planet. As we get involved with fighting for the poor and bringing a biblical agenda to society, we will begin to have a voice again.

But we can't merely talk about these problems and issues. We have to be a positive part of the solution, and we have a great opportunity because governments are realising that the cost of healthcare and education is prohibitive, so they're inviting the church to play a role as it did in previous years. We must not miss this opportunity to play our part, to reconnect with society in a way we haven't done in the past 200 years.

Sometimes we have to *be* good news before we earn the right to *preach* the good news. This is true for all our friendships and relationships – we want to be a blessing and not just talk about God's blessings – but it's also true if we want people in the wider community to become Christians.

What happens when you bring worship, evangelism and justice together?

Some years ago Steve Chalke spoke at Soul Survivor and he brought with him the biggest truck I've ever seen. As he preached, he challenged us as part of our worship to go out of the meeting hall, back to our tents and to return with an item of clothing we would like to offer to God to be taken to homeless people in London. The idea was not to bring something we didn't really need or want any more, but to sacrifice something we had brought with us, not realising this would be asked of us. Steve asked that we worship as we went as a reminder that this was another expression of our love for God.

So the band continued to play as 6,000 kids filed from the meeting room back to their tents. Gradually the empty hall began to fill up again and huge queues formed outside by the lorry as the young people offered their clothes and belongings. Some cried as they gave over the things they valued and all the while songs of love and devotion were being sung. All of a sudden it hit me that this was an amazing expression of worship that Steve had challenged us to offer, and how this seemed to me to be the worship God required: not only to sing the songs of devotion but to mean them so much that we would be willing to put that love into action and sacrifice whatever He asked of us.

Of course, this expression of worship wasn't without its issues (some parents weren't exactly thrilled to find out their children had given away birthday presents and we were surprised at how many 'gave' items that didn't belong to them), but the majority of people there gave something they loved as a token of their devotion to God.

This was an act of worship to God; it was evangelism, because every person on the streets of London who received a new pair of trainers or a warm jumper knew it came from Christians, and it was an act of justice to share what we had with others in need.

Being good news

In 2004 we ran 'Soul in the City', where 11,600 young people descended on our capital city to love and serve those who live and work there. It was a worship festival in that we worshipped in song each morning and evening, and then worshipped on the streets during the days. This worship took many shapes and forms, from gardening projects, painting over graffiti, decorating youth and community centres to running holiday clubs for children.

The idea was to serve people with no strings attached – there was no condition that we would do something for them if they would only listen to a five-minute presentation of the gospel or come to an event we were putting on. But what happens when you offer something for nothing? People want to know why. The last thing the city of London expected was for over 10,000 young people to come and pay to serve them for nothing. We couldn't get away from talking about Jesus because our actions caused them to ask questions. They wanted to know what would make a young person in today's self-centred culture give up part of their summer holiday and pay for the privilege of clearing up the litter of complete strangers who live hundreds of miles away. There was no other answer people could give – there was only one reason we were doing this: Jesus. We found that people were much more open to hearing about Jesus once they'd seen Him in action. We could say that Jesus loved them because we'd demonstrated it.

We estimated that 6,000 people made commitments to Jesus through the various projects. Lasting change was brought to communities, smiles were put on people's faces, hope was put back in people's hearts and many thousands were left with a lasting impression of young people serving in the name of Jesus. Not rattling a collection tin in His name. Not someone preaching at them and telling them they were sinners. Just the people of God loving and serving Him and them.

The key to revival?

It can't just be about one-off missions. This has to form part of our daily life. If we want to see revival we need to bring all these elements of worship, evangelism and justice together, realising that a life of passionate worship of God means first and foremost spending time with Him, loving Him and growing in our relationship with Him, as well as feeding the hungry, standing up for those who suffer injustice, identifying with them in their pain and suffering and being willing to stand alongside them and fight on their behalf. We should be preaching the gospel at all times, speaking and acting out God's love to a hurt and broken world.

We have to realise that to tell people about Jesus but leave them starving to death or wasting away in prison when they have been falsely accused is offensive to God. Equally, to meet their physical needs and ignore their spiritual ones is appalling, as whatever improvement we can hope to bring to their life on earth, it is nothing in comparison to being reconciled with their heavenly Father.

It's unlikely to be a glamorous task. The vast majority of us will never have films made about our lives, enter a room to rapturous applause, be followed by a news crew or be asked for our autograph at the end of a day's work. God never promised us any of those things. As we fix our eyes on Him we remember that while there is a place for big dreams and wild adventures, worshipping God is about making good choices every day, even in the seemingly small decisions we make.

What God did say is that He would see each act we do in His name and He would notice each good choice we make. It may be that no one on earth ever knows all that you do in the name of Jesus, but when you stand before your heavenly Father you will be sure to hear the words, 'Well done, good and faithful servant.'

Therefore I urge you, brothers [and sisters] in Christ, in view of God's overwhelming love and mercy, to offer your bodies [your hearts, your minds, your voices, your hands, your feet, your bank accounts, your shopping decisions, your internet access, your homes and your possessions] as living sacrifices [to do with as he will]. For this is a holy and pleasing spiritual act of worship to the Lord your God. (Adapted from Romans 12:1)

Bibliography

Bono on Bono: Conversations with Michka Assayas, Hodder & Stoughton 2005.

Richard Foster, *Celebration of Discipline*, Hodder & Stoughton 1980, 1989.

Pete Greig and Dave Roberts, *Red Moon Rising: The Story of 24–7 Prayer*, Survivor 2003.

Gary A. Haugen, *Good News about Injustice: A Witness of Courage in a Hurting World*, InterVarsity Press 1999.

Brother Lawrence (translated by E.M. Blaiklock), *The Practice of the Presence of God*, Hodder & Stoughton 1981.

David Ruis, *The Worship God Is Seeking*, Regal Books 2004.

Survivor books...receive as you read

Wasteland: Mike Pilavachi (£5.99)

With honesty and wit, Mike helps us to understand – and
even relish – those difficult times in our lives when our
dreams are unrealised and our spirituality feels dry and life-
less by drawing from characters in the Old and New
Testament.

SoulintheCity DVD (£7.99)

This 30 minute DVD captures the energy, enthusiasm and
the hearts of people and churches who worked together to
reach out to their local communities. Bonus features include
Louie Giglio's inspiring teaching and worship with 15,000
people from Trafalgar Square, with Tim Hughes & Mark
Beswick.

Urban Legends (£5.99)

With stories from delegates, residents and Partner churches
plus features from those who organized it, this sizzling pro-
duction will give you unique insight into how 750 churches
were mobilized to work together, host 12,000 young people
from around the UK and collaborate together in a unique
outreach.

The Truth Will Set You Free: Beth Redman (£5.99)

With insight and humour, Beth helps young women to find
God's answers to the big questions and struggles in their
lives. Thousands of teenage girls have come to trust Beth
Redman's powerful and relevant teaching through her
packed seminars at Soul Survivor.

Passion for Your Name: Tim Hughes (£6.99)

Timely and timeless advice for today's worship leader and
worship band. Tim Hughes looks first at the reasons why we
worship God, why we need to get our hearts right with him,
choosing song lists, musical dynamics, small group worship,
and the art of songwriting.

www.survivor.co.uk

survivor

Survivor books...receive as you read

City Changing Prayer: Debra & Frank Green (£6.99)
Imagine a regular city-wide gathering of Christians united and focused in prayer. Imagine the crime rate falling; teenagers praying; people beginning to believe that there is something in this thing called prayer.

Eden: called to the Streets: Matt Wilson (£6.99)
Matt Wilson tracks the story of Eden where followers of Jesus are moving out of their comfort zones and planting their homes and souls in urban community. They choose to live out their lives in the face of some of the highest rates of crime, social deprivation, drug and alcohol abuse and unemployment.

Diary of a Dangerous Vision: Andy Hawthorne (£6.99)
This is the story of Andy Hawthorne's dramatic conversion and the adventure of an ever-growing group of Christians set to take Christ into the most tough urban areas. Reading this book will leave you challenged and inspired.

24-7 Prayer Manual (£9.99)
People are praying 24 hours a day, 7 days a week in countries around the world. This concise but detailed guide will help churches, youth groups, Christian Unions and groups of churches set up prayer rooms for one day, one week or one month. It's full of creative, low cost ideas that will help make the life changing prayer room experience accessible to everyone.

survivor

www.survivor.co.uk